About Gerald Benedict

After an education conferred by a variety of schools, Gerald Benedict was commissioned in the Royal Marines and served in Sierra Leone with the Royal West African Frontier Force. He then read Divinity at the University of London, and studied for a postgraduate diploma in Philosophy at the Graduate School of Ecumenical Studies, University of Geneva, and a Ph.D. in Philosophy at the Open University. After teaching in universities and colleges of higher education, he now lives in France and writes full-time. He has won awards for a novel, several short stories, and radio drama for the BBC World Service. Previous books include *The Watkins Dictionary of Religious and Secular Faiths*, *The Maya Prophecies for 2012*, and several anthologies in the Watkins "Sacred Texts" series.

THE FIVE-MINUTE PHILOSOPHER

80 UNQUESTIONABLY GOOD ANSWERS
TO 80 UNANSWERABLE BIG QUESTIONS

GERALD BENEDICT

WATKINS PUBLISHING
LONDON

This edition first published in the UK and USA 2011 by
Watkins Publishing, Sixth Floor, Castle House,
75–76 Wells Street, London W1T 3QH

Design and typography copyright © Watkins Publishing 2011

Text copyright © Gerald Benedict 2011

1 3 5 7 9 10 8 6 4 2

Designed by Jerry Goldie Graphic Design

Printed and bound by Imago in China

British Library Cataloguing-in-Publication Data Available
Library of Congress Cataloging-in-Publication Data Available

ISBN: 978-1-78028-010-3

www.watkinspublishing.co.uk

Distributed in the USA and Canada by Sterling Publishing Co., Inc.
387 Park Avenue South, New York, NY 10016-8810

For information about custom editions, special sales, premium and
corporate purchases, please contact Sterling Special Sales
Department at 800-805-5489 or specialsales@sterlingpub.com

Contents

Introduction

" *Human reason has this peculiar fate,*
that in one species of its knowledge it
is burdened by questions which, as
prescribed by the very nature of reason
itself, it is not able to ignore, but
which, as transcending all its power,
it is also not able to answer. "

IMMANUEL KANT (1724–1804)

No one can live without asking questions. The need to know, whether prompted by necessity or curiosity, has its own reason for existing: it is an inherent function of the mind. Asking a question and searching for the answer was, for the first human beings, a survival technique; for us it's the process by which we can occupy our time on Earth in the most meaningful way. It is, of course, important to ask the right questions, as a whole lifetime can be spent pursuing answers to the wrong ones. As James Thurber (1894–1961) remarked, "It is better to know some of the questions than all of the answers."

Asking questions begins in early childhood and continues for as long as we live. Questions are the mind's windows onto the undiscovered world, the link between the known and the unknown. Most of the ones that crowd our day are simply a means of gathering information and facts: "How are you?" "What time is it?" "Can you tell me how to ...?" The important questions, however, are about why we *have* a day, and why we have the need to ask questions in the first place. Most of our learning is in the spaces between questions and answers, and here too is the framework of most teaching. This is the Socratic method, a dialectic that operates by posing one point of view against another, and pursuing the debate by querying the answers to the questions that are posed. This is the "on the other hand, think about it this way ..." method of arriving at truth. Socrates (469–399 BC) was known as "the midwife of men's thoughts", and each question we ask, or are asked, is the midwife aiding the birth of new knowledge and perceptions. New ideas, the first fruits of our minds, are sown by questions and harvested by reflection.

The questions considered in this book are not about facts and information. They are the kind of question for which an answer is not readily available, and looking for the answer is more like a journey of exploration than a browse through an encyclopedia. The territory to be explored is oneself, and what is required is intro-spection, combined with open-mindedness; self-knowledge, combined with a willingness to relinquish our set patterns of thought. Sooner or later we find ourselves thinking about these conundrums. Usually we are simply too busy to dwell on them: there are other demands, other priorities, all necessary and justi-fiable. But one of the shortcomings of our present lives is that we fail to see the need for even brief periods of solitude in which, alone with ourselves, we can dwell on challenging questions, and by reflection remould our lives. The French philosopher Simone Weil (1909–1943) believed that "for every person there should be enough room, enough freedom to plan the use of one's time, the opportunity to reach even higher levels of attention, some solitude, some silence." At such moments, we move from what she termed the personal to the impersonal. From the "I" with which we identify our fears and needs, our ambitions and hopes, we achieve a temporary liberation, progressing to the "I" which breaks free of our self-preoccupation to reach for "higher levels of attention", where we know ourselves to be part of a greater "whole". Some of the questions offered may require a response that is a form of meditative quietude.

No real answers can ever be given to the questions. What might seem like answers are merely a summary of the salient issues. A truism it may be, but for every answer there's a question – in fact, many questions. And in thinking about the responses given, the reader may well formulate a question that is more important or better focused. Outside the realm of fact and information there are no instant answers and pondering the questions will take time, self-reflection, honesty, even courage. What at best may happen in the process of browsing this book is a rearrangement of the reader's thinking, the putting together of ideas already formulated with new ideas suddenly perceived, in a new pattern. The mind is like a kaleidoscope into which new shapes and colours are introduced to those already present, so as to spin off entirely new motifs and configurations for our ideas and perceptions. Thinking about these questions, right thinking, will take a person beyond the territory of what they already know. If, in the passage quoted on page 3, Kant is right about reason being able neither to ignore nor to answer our most pressing questions, it follows that considering possible answers may require reason to be transcended.

The questions in this book are arranged under the following headings.

Knowledge: What we know is put together from many sources and acquired by a variety of means. At its simplest, knowledge is an addition of facts or expertise, drawn from education and experience which can be either practical (knowing "how") or theoretical (knowing "that"). It can be general or specialized, and it includes our responses to abstract ideas and the insights drawn from them. For something to be known, it has to be true, and be underpinned by what Plato (c. 428–c. 347 BC) called "justified true belief". The difference between knowledge and belief (which has its own section: see below) is important: knowledge is mostly concerned with certainty, belief with trust. It is in the nature of mind to acquire knowledge, while it is a state of mind that holds beliefs. Using knowledge as a marker of what we do not know motivates us to know even more. The questions under this heading range across the nature of both knowledge and the knower.

Self: The "self", as an existing entity, is elusive and difficult to locate, and it seems to resist clear philosophical or psychological definition. We can say that a sense of self is the knowing and responding subject that remains constant through the ever-changing landscape of our mental and physical states which are, nevertheless, owned by the self. Constant the self may be, in the sense that it's always there and that we are always conscious of it, but because it's only evident in relationships, be that with people, things, the environment, nature and so on, what we are no less aware of is the self changing in response to these different stimuli. Whether in relation to religious faith, agnosticism, atheism or secularism, the self carries a sense of its own uniqueness, and by extension we arrive at the idea that we each have a "true" or "essential self". This may be the same as, or similar to, Plato's concept of the soul, or the thinking substance. Or it may be the "I" of René Descartes (1596–1650): "I think, therefore I am." Or it may be the "ego" of Sigmund Freud (1856–1939). However, the use of the word "self" to represent something incorporeal is thought by some philosophers to be obsolete. David Hume (1711–1776), for example, denied that we could be "intimately conscious of what we call our self", since the experiences that make us aware of what we think of as self are constantly changing. Hume continues, "If any impression gives rise to the idea of self, that impression must continue invariably the same, through the whole course of our lives; since self is supposed to exist after that manner. But there is no impression constant and invariable." The questions address these and other themes.

Cosmos: There is growing interest on all questions related to the cosmos, particularly in connection with its origins, and the beginnings of life on Earth. This interest in origins has given rise to speculation about the possibility of life existing elsewhere, and while this is unlikely within our own solar system, the hypothesis that there are countless other solar systems allows that a form of life may exist lightyears away from Earth. Stephen Hawking (b.1942) confided in us that "all my life, I have been fascinated by the big questions that face us, and have tried to find scientific answers to them." Apart from these "big questions", others, equally meaningful, seek to understand how our awareness of current cosmology affects our self-perception, and how "on Earth" we can possibly fit into the greater scheme. Paul Ricœur (1913–2005) made the point that, "on a cosmic scale, our life is insignificant, yet this brief period when we appear in the world is the time in which all meaningful questions arise." Some of those "meaningful questions" are offered under this heading.

Humankind: Hamlet called man "the paragon of animals", but Charles Darwin (1809–1882) noted that "man with all his noble qualities ... still bears in his bodily frame the indelible stamp of his lowly origin." Our understanding of humankind is still caught in the tension between creationists and biological evolutionists, while intelligent design, once thought to be a viable bridge between the two, no longer has credit. As highly developed as we are from those "lowly origins", humankind still seems to have insurmountable problems, especially those concerned with how to live in peace with each other, and how to live responsibly with regard to the Earth's environment. There are many factors that distinguish us from other animals, but Eric Fromm (1900–1980) was undoubtedly right in observing that "man is the only animal for whom his own existence is a problem he has to solve." The problem of our existence revolves around whether or not life has meaning and purpose, either one that is built in and determined by our genetics, or one that we discover for ourselves and carry back to life. The human animal is complex, not just in terms of its biology but also in terms of its faculties, such as intelligence, mind, imagination and creativity. Despite its extraordinary evolution and its genius in every field, humankind senses that at the very heart of what we are there is something missing. The questions ranging across these themes will, perhaps, confirm this aphorism by Friedrich Nietzsche (1844–1900): "He who has a why to live can bear almost any how."

Spirituality: The sense of lack referred to above concerns what has always been the most strongly debated issue about humankind: whether or not, within our physical make-up, there is an element – call it self, or soul, or some other numinous thing – that is naturally given to spiritual perception and to transcending the material world. The entire history of the human race carries with it the quest for "the other", a quest Francis of Assisi (1181–1226) expressed with commendable simplicity: "what you are looking for is what is looking." It is hoped that the recent and energetic evangelism by atheists can remain in creative dialogue with those who, whether by faith or experience, believe themselves not to be "human beings having a spiritual experience … but spiritual beings having a human experience" (Pierre Teilhard de Chardin, 1881–1955). We are not, necessarily, concerned here with the theology and dogma of established religions. Spirituality does not rest either on the authority credited to textual sources of religion or on the conservatism of the received tradition; rather, it addresses the miracle of the mundane. Alan Watts (1915–1973) put it this way: "Zen does not confuse spirituality with thinking about God while one is peeling potatoes. Zen spirituality is just to peel the potatoes." This section is a watershed, over which the spiritual and secular rivers of life may, perhaps, divide.

Religion: It has been said, anonymously, that "Philosophy is questions that may never be answered. Religion is answers that may never be questioned," and it is this dogmatism, backed up by forceful authority, that has always been religion's greatest problem. Religion, representing both the established expression of faith, and doctrine as the measure of what "should" be believed, has been the source of both the greatest wrongdoing and the greatest good. It has satisfied people's lust for power and control, but also it has been the means for selfless service to others. Through the wars it has incited, and the punishments it has inflicted for heresy, it has caused appalling suffering; but its compassion and social conscience have initiated the education and medical care of millions across the world. It has destroyed entire cultures, yet has inspired some of the greatest art on Earth. Within the parameters of religion's orthodoxy and conservatism, uncountable numbers have been brought to a sincere belief; but as free thinkers, many have had to break out of their received tradition in order to find their own living faith. As the comedian Lenny Bruce (1925–1966) put it, "Every day people are straying away from the church and going back to God," and this says something positive about religion, since, as G.K. Chesterton (1874–1936) believed, "it is the test of a good religion whether you can joke about it."

Belief. Earlier, the distinction was made between knowledge and belief, and it was noted that belief implies trust. The term "faith" also implies trust, and in statements such as "I believe in you" or "I believe everything will be all right", the two concepts are interchangeable. However, they do have shades of difference. Belief usually applies to ideas, a system of thought that is represented by, for example, a creed or a secular manifesto. Faith is usually associated with absolute rather than relative truths, and customarily relates to spirituality. It is possible to believe in something we do not know, because we sense or intuit that it is right; faith is the disposition to commit to that intuition. Belief hints at confidence, while faith implies risk – we speak of "the leap of faith". Faith relates to the unprecedented – for example, the first person to achieve something, whether conquering Everest or flying across the Atlantic, had faith, and demonstrated that what they did was possible. Those following them believed they could do the same thing, thanks to the faith of the pioneer. Ground-breaking faith is rare, and it has been the faith of a few that has inspired the belief of many. For the purposes of the questions given in this section, it is not necessary to hold these terms apart, since each of us can determine our own meaningful usage. Isaac Asimov (1920–1992) used both words to express his opinion that "there is no belief, however foolish, that will not gather its faithful adherents who will defend it to the death."

Behaviour. The "best" way to live is determined by the mores and laws of our society. These are directed to ensure that, so far as is possible, we live together peaceably, each giving respect to the rights and property of the other. What form the laws and conventions take depends on the kind of society we want, although it is rare, outside of philosophy, for anyone, or any governing group, to address this question, not just in terms of law and constitution, but also in terms of education. Our society has not been determined, it has developed, somewhat like a garden, under the hands of ever-changing designers. But unlike a garden, the general ambience of Western society is not one of quietude, but of stress, anxiety and uncertainty. The causes of this are various, ranging across ecological, economic and political problems. We have a sense of government struggling to hold our civilization together. David Émile Durkheim (1858–1917), the French sociologist, argued that human behaviour was determined by what he called "social fact", writing: "A social fact is every way of acting, fixed or not, capable of exercising on the individual an external constraint." How we behave is "coerced" by laws and regulations, and Durkheim suggested that the more immature the society, the more complicated its legal and regulatory systems will be. Albert Schweitzer (1875–1965) suggested a far simpler formula but one that would require a high degree of personal and social maturity: "Ethics, too, are nothing but reverence for life. That is what gives me the fundamental principle of morality, namely, that the good consists in maintaining, promoting, and enhancing life, and that destroying, injuring and limiting life are evil."

Asking questions is a means of becoming free. True reflection on questions, especially those for which there are no absolute or clear answers, is a means of breaking out of the confines of what we already know, and from what has moulded and conditioned the way we think. It is an opportunity to break away from the dictatorship of dogma, custom, and the seemingly unquestionable opinions of specialists in whatever field we happen to live and work. Our freedom to think for ourselves is hard won, and we should use it to "love the questions" and to "live the answers", as the poet Rainer Maria Rilke (1875–1926) encouraged us to do: "Have patience with everything unresolved in your heart and try to love the questions themselves. Don't search for answers now, because you would not be able to live them. And the point is to live everything."

I

Knowledge

"The only good is knowledge and the only evil is ignorance."

SOCRATES (*c*.469–399 BC)

"The opposite of a true statement is a false statement, but the opposite of a profound truth can be another profound truth."

NIELS BOHR (1885–1962)

What is knowledge?

What we know is the sum total of everything our minds have absorbed and retained since birth. It is what enables us to relate to the world, and to be intelligently in contact with everything our senses receive. Our accumulated knowledge enables us to recognize, respond, categorize and organize the information given by the hugely complex stimuli to which we are constantly exposed. It is a storehouse of data recalled by memory, itself activated by the need, or desire, to respond to an ever-changing landscape of incentives. Put briefly, knowledge is information acquired by experience. Empiricism is the theory that all knowledge is based solely on observation, experiment and deduction. An alternative way of thinking is Idealism, a group of philosophical theories taking the view that what we call the external world is created by the mind. While recognizing that material things exist, idealists argue that their nature is dependent on our perceptions.

There is a difference between the kind of thing we know *about*, and the kind of thing we know because we have observed it, or done it. The former might be termed "referred knowledge", the latter "practical knowledge". We know about Mount Everest without ever having seen it directly; we know how to transplant a heart, or play a musical instrument, because we have acquired the skill through training. These forms of knowledge overlap, since we also know *about* heart transplants and making music.

The simplest forms of knowledge are attached to facts, the names of things, the unambiguous world of nouns and the way we differentiate using adjectives. Such facts, whether historical dates, the names of our family and friends, the distinguishing features of birds, or the parts that make up a car's engine, are learned both formally and informally. Examples of more complex forms of knowledge are concepts and ideas. We each have a personal sense of beauty, of what is "good" both aesthetically and morally, and each of us is attached, however vaguely, to a political ideal and some of us also to a religious belief. Our gradual laying down of the knowledge that these beliefs or responses require enables us to make value judgments on which all the choices we constantly make are based. Knowing ourselves is arguably our most significant learning curve. Gradually, we learn to know what we like and dislike, what we value or discount, what we must learn and do to realize our individual potential. Self-knowledge is acquired in relation to our environment, to things and to people. However, it can only be subjective. More reliable is our knowledge of others, as this can be tested against evidence that is more readily available and verifiable: such knowledge is reciprocal and mutually enlightening. Lucilius (c.160s–103/2 BC) wrote: "Knowledge is not knowledge until someone else knows that one knows."

Wisdom can be thought of as a deep understanding of everything a person knows, applied to people, situations, choices and judgments. Confucius (551–479 BC) said that wisdom is learned in three stages, "first, by reflection, which is noblest; second by imitation, which is easiest; and third by experience, which is bitterest."

Is there a limit to what we can know and understand?

In an age when scientists are looking for the one theory that will, at the same time, tell us about the origin of the universe and give us a single, unifying formula for all of life, the assumption is that, potentially, we can know everything there is to be known. In *A Brief History of Time,* Stephen Hawking (b.1942) makes it clear that the goal is "nothing less than a complete description of the universe we live in", but for the present the problem has to be broken down into partial theories, such as relativity and quantum mechanics, before it is possible to see if they can be put together as one.

Probably most of us are content to leave the ultimate questions to the cosmologists and astrophysicists. Today, humankind has amassed more knowledge than ever before, but what we have learned has been a collective process: countless numbers of people from every age and culture have contributed to the sum total of our knowledge. We have, to parody Jung's phrase, a collective consciousness, which despite the extraordinary range and depth of information acquired falls a long way short of omniscience. Even if we start with the premise that, potentially, there are no limits to what we can know, it is likely that our experience will tell us otherwise; or, put differently, the possibility of knowing and understanding everything is frustrated by other factors such as time, the quality and size of the human brain, and the demands of the knowledge we already have that requires radical adaptation and change.

Our sole working tool is the brain, and even with millions of them working together, the way in which the brain functions

*" If a little knowledge is dangerous, where
is the man who has so much as to be out
of danger? "*

T.H. HUXLEY (1825–1895)

determines what we achieve in every field. The brain is a living
organism which, like any other, is subject to physical problems. It
is not autonomous, since it requires energy to function properly,
and it is dependent on the well-being of the whole body, specifically the senses, for the information it receives and processes.
Malfunctions of the eyes or ears, for example, influence the quality
of the signals to the brain.

Clearly, there is a limit to what we can know and understand at
any one time. If we eventually do gain complete knowledge, say, of
the origins of the universe, the process will probably take a very
considerable amount of time. It is hard to imagine what will
happen once that goal has been achieved, since it is the quest for
knowledge that has led to the growth of civilizations. So basic is
this quest that it can be argued that the need to know is a driver in
human evolution. We cannot leave this discussion without
referring to the knowledge that has been lost as different civilizations have arisen and declined. If we are to know everything, then
recovering that knowledge must be part of the learning process.
For the time being, omniscience is a quality that is, perhaps, best
left with God.

Learning is a humbling process, and on the subject of knowing and understanding the vastness and origins of the universe we may well find ourselves agreeing with Socrates (c.469–399 BC): "All I know is that I know nothing."

How can we know that what we know is right?

Philosophers have long debated how we can be confident that the knowledge we acquire is accurate. Normally we don't need to put everything to the test, we know that 2+2 = 4, that tomatoes are red, and that Great Britain is an island off the northwest coast of Europe. If there is doubt or argument, such facts are easily verifiable. But in the process of acquiring new knowledge we need to have confidence that it is correct, and there may be times when to question, rather than to accept what we have read or heard, can be useful. Even if it is obvious that something is right, it is sometimes necessary to put the matter to the test ourselves.

Verifying whether or not any proposition is correct can be a complex and subtle process, and much depends on the methods we use to corroborate the statement. Usually, we test the rightness of an opinion according to our own observation and experience. If what we hear accords with what we have already discovered, then we are likely to accept it as being right. The "rightness" of what we know is not necessarily determined by the number of people who hold the same opinion: the majority can be profoundly wrong. Thus, as a method of verification, testing the correctness of an opinion against the number of people holding it is not a reliable procedure. Another method is to consider the meaning of words. C.E.M. Joad (1891–1953), a philosopher and broadcaster who, during World War Two, participated in the popular BBC radio programme *The Brains Trust*, became famous for his catchphrase, "It all depends on what you mean by ...", which prefaced his answers to the questions put to the panel. Although overplayed, Joad's qualification is important. To know that what we know is right depends entirely on our use and interpretation of language. The subject of the verification of knowledge was a central theme of logical positivism, a form of philosophy established by the Vienna Circle in the 1920s and 1930s, its two most famous proponents being Bertrand Russell (1872–1970) and Ludwig Wittgenstein (1889–1951). Both were concerned with the meanings of words and with the structure of language as a method of determining whether or not a proposition is "right". Wittgenstein argued that we can do nothing without language, that all our thoughts are linguistically contrived and are pictures of reality. He described reality as the totality of facts about the world, so that to talk of anything outside verifiable reality, such as the existence of God, is meaningless. Since the concept is not a part of the factual reality of the world, there is no suitable language for it and thus nothing for the mind to picture.

The Greek Skeptic philosophers claimed that knowledge can never be sure: it can never amount to certainty, but only to probability. They had a word for this view: "acatalepsy". It sounds, just a little, like a medical condition.

Is there really such a thing as truth?

The previous question, about how we corroborate whether or not something we know is right, inevitably touches on the concept of "truth". Literally, for something to be "true" it would need to conform to fact or reality. "Right" and "true" are words that run closely together, but they are not synonymous. A statement can be right, or true, or both. If it's true, it is also correct, but if a statement is correct it will not necessarily be true. I can demonstrate that I'm not on the moon or in Antarctica or Tashkent; I can argue that, not being in those places, I'm elsewhere, and that if I'm elsewhere, I'm not here. The statement, as a play on words, is correct, but it's not true.

When we first consider whether or not something is true, we can qualify it by saying, against the strongest argument, that it's true or not true "for me". It has been said that a person with an experience is never at the mercy of a person with an argument: if I claim to have a headache, no one can justify contradicting me.

❝ Jesus answered, '… for this I have come into the world – to bear witness to the truth. Everyone who is of the truth hears my voice.' Pilate said to him, 'What is truth?' ❞

(JOHN 18:37–38)

This raises the question of whether something can be both true and entirely subjective, and the further question as to whether something unverifiable can be held to be true. It is important to take into account that we can know with certainty that something is true, even though it cannot be proved. I might know who broke my neighbour's window, but have no means of proving the fact.

The quotation displayed on the opposite page defines Jesus' manifesto: he has come to us to bear witness to the truth. To be a witness requires the necessary knowledge and authority, and four chapters earlier, John records that Jesus claimed *to be* the truth (John 14:6). But to what truth was Jesus witness? However we understand and interpret Jesus' teachings, the truth he represented can be thought of as absolute, or ultimate, requiring us to think in terms of the meaning and purpose of life in an eternal context. All religions bear witness to absolute truth, a notion that takes us beyond the relative truth of reality as defined by Wittgenstein into a realm he would regard as meaningless. Werner Heisenberg, the German theoretical physicist (1901–1976), said that "it will never be possible by pure reason to arrive at some absolute truth."

Do we, then, have to allow for something other than pure reason that may give us access to truths that are not part of what we think of as the "real" world? While not given credence by philosophers of logic, there are many who claim to grasp "greater" truths by means of contemplation, intuition, faith and enlightenment. Most religious traditions advise their adherents to turn inwards, suggesting that what Jesus bore witness to is to be found within ourselves. The Zen Buddhist master Dogen

Zenji (1200–1253) asked, "If you cannot find the truth right where you are, where else do you expect to find it?" Some will be more comfortable with the assertion of Gustave Flaubert (1821–1880) that "there is no truth. There is only perception." Others may discover, like Sri Ramana Maharshi (1879–1950), that "there is no Truth. There is only the truth within each moment."

What can we know about the future?

Since antiquity, the future has mystified and beguiled people. We have always wanted to know what will happen in the months and years ahead, and our attempts to find out have engendered an extraordinary assortment of methods and techniques. These have included reading the entrails of animals, consulting oracles, interpreting omens, reading the Tarot, palmistry, dream interpretation, and astrology. Such methods work within supernatural or paranormal parameters and, unsurprisingly, have been subject to scientific scepticism. What is gleaned of the future by these means is probably closer to speculation than knowledge.

More rational methods of anticipating what will happen involve what are called probability theories, and for these mathematics, quantum physics and computer models are used. By such means it is becoming possible, for example, to predict the likelihood of an earthquake or the eruption of a volcano. NASA has been able to give warning that in 2012 we shall experience unprecedented sunspot activity which will have knock-on effects on Earth. Demography enables us to know the extent and rate at which the world's population will increase, and in which countries this is likely to be most pronounced. Such statistics, in turn, indicate what must be done to feed the increasing population. Observation of the world's environment has made us aware of global warming, and the long-term effects of this, it is thought, might put our planet at risk. In the ever-changing world of politics, an interesting and much used form of statistical prediction is opinion polls, which try to indicate the outcome of an election or referendum. Similarly, in business, particularly for globalized companies, huge databases of statistics endeavour to predict the changing fortunes of markets.

However, while it is of comfort to know that radio-telescopes are gathering information that might indicate the likelihood of the Earth coming into collision with a massive meteorite, and that the confidence of investors and share-holders is justified by expert projections of supply and demand and other commercial variables, these matters are not of immediate daily concern to the majority of people. Most would settle for knowing what is going to happen to them this time next week, or even tomorrow afternoon: they'd be glad to know which horse is going to win the next race, which football teams will win, lose or draw. More importantly, we would all like to know if our good health will be sustained, or, if we are ill, what the chances are for our recovery. From professional sources we are given clear indications of these aspects of our future, but in the medium and long term those wanting to know what will happen to themselves, their families and their friends must still have recourse to horoscopes, fortune tellers and prophets.

Peter Drucker (1909–2005) is surely right in saying, "the best way to predict the future is to create it," but we cannot know if what we create will be sustainable.

What do we "need" to know?

In one sense this is an open question, the answer depending on time, place and circumstance; in another sense, the answer is focused on our need to survive physically. Around 100,000 years ago, we'd have needed to know how to construct a shelter, how to cover our bodies, how to hunt and forage for food, how to make and sustain a fire, and how to survive physical trauma and illness. The complexity of a highly developed society requires specialization, and it is this that has gradually removed us from the need to know how to survive. Today, what we need to know in order to survive physically has been given over to others – the construction industry, the producers and distributors of food, those with medical skills, the emergency services and the armed forces. In what is called the "Third World", people still need to know how to survive physically, and although helped by aid agencies, remain directly responsible for their own well-being. In the Western world what most of us need to know is how to survive financially.

The military principle of the "need to know" requires that just sufficient knowledge is given to carry out the job in hand, the point being that in a military context what we don't know we can't divulge under duress. It could be said that our lives are similarly structured. Because we rely on others for our physical survival, we need to know only what is necessary to pursue our careers and, arguably, we may not know as much as we should. In broad terms, what we need to know is determined by the gaps in our knowledge. But of equal importance is the kind of knowledge that enables us to form our priorities and our sense of values, since these in turn determine the kinds of decisions and judgments we make during the course of our everyday lives.

We need, of course, to know ourselves, and some would say, to know God in whatever form he addresses us most meaningfully. But we don't need to break our heads to know the ultimate meaning of everything, only that life does have a meaning and purpose, even though that may be something we bring to it ourselves. Perhaps, less obviously, the most important thing we need to know is how to change in a constantly and rapidly changing world. Charles

" 'I want to know, for example, why beauty exists,' she [Gabrielle] said, 'why nature continues to contrive it, and what is the link between the life of a tree and its beauty, and what connects the mere existence of the sea or a lightning storm with the feelings these things inspire in us? If God does not exist, if these things are not unified into one metaphorical system, then why do they retain for us such symbolic power?' "

ANNE RICE (B.1941)

Darwin (1809–1882) stated it thus: "It is not the strongest of the species that survives, not the most intelligent that survives. It is the one that is the most adaptable to change."

Does great knowledge imply great wisdom?

Philosophers have usually regarded wisdom as the capacity to make the best use of knowledge, and in all cultures it has been personified, most familiarly in the West as the goddess "Sophia", in which form wisdom has been depicted in art and poetry. The Greek Sophists offered to teach wisdom professionally; the Old Testament includes six "Wisdom" books; and Philo (20 BC–AD 50) the Hellenistic Jewish philosopher, used the term *logos* to harmonize Platonic and Jewish concepts of wisdom, an idea taken up in the prologue to John's Gospel. In all forms of Christianity, and in the Jewish Kabbalah, Sophia, as Holy Wisdom, has been central to mysticism. For Buddhists, the Sanskrit term *prajna*, translated as "wisdom", refers to the foundational concept of the Mahayana tradition, understood as immediately experienced intuition, or an intuitive apprehension. It is beyond conceptualization, the core of insight into emptiness, which is the true nature of reality. As such, wisdom is equated with enlightenment, and is one of the signs of buddhahood.

The debate about the relationship between knowledge and wisdom frequently sets the two in opposition, but at the level of meaning there is no conflict. A person can be very knowledgeable but lack wisdom, but if wise will be very knowledgeable. Knowledge is something learned, wisdom is acquired by experience, and while they are inextricably related, wisdom, in some ways, holds itself apart, as Herman Hesse (1877–1962) noted: "Knowledge can be communicated, but not wisdom. One can find it, live it, be fortified by it, do wonders through it, but one cannot communicate and teach it."

Wisdom and knowledge both require understanding, and each is related to intelligence, but their value and their role in life are in tension. In education, knowledge amounts to absorbing and memorizing an uncountable number of facts: the need to know *about* things is indispensable for success in the long series of tests and examinations faced by students. We are taught to apply knowledge, but this is far more about the application of knowledge to knowledge than the application of knowledge to life. The measure of a person's worth is determined not just by the extent of their knowledge, but also by how quickly it can be recalled – testing how much a person knows is the purpose of hugely

. . . .

❝ Wisdom allows nothing to be good that will not be so forever; no man to be happy but he that needs no other happiness than what he has within himself; no man to be great or powerful that is not master of himself. ❞

SENECA THE YOUNGER (*c.*3 BC–AD 65)

popular radio and TV games. The results are extraordinary, and we sit back and marvel at people's prodigious memories and the speed at which they can recall what St Augustine (AD354–430) termed "the rational knowledge of temporal things".

How, then, can we recognize in a person the difference between rational knowledge and real wisdom? We may hear someone say something profound, or offer advice we know to be judicious, but to be confident that a person is *consistently wise* requires a relationship, as between a pupil and teacher, or a disciple and a guru, and in such a relationship we come to realize that wisdom draws on extensive knowledge and experience. Wisdom does not reside only in the mind's faculties of reason and intelligence, it also draws on emotion, will and spirituality; nevertheless, wisdom always remains grounded in knowledge. But only the wise listener will recognize the wisdom heard: "It requires wisdom to understand wisdom: the music is nothing if the audience is deaf" (Walter Lippmann, 1889–1974).

2

Self

*"This above all: to thine own self
    be true,*

*And it must follow, as the night
    the day,*

*Thou canst not then be false to
    any man "*

WILLIAM SHAKESPEARE (1564–1616), FROM *HAMLET*

*"Who has not sat, afraid,
before his own heart's curtain? "*

RAINER MARIA RILKE (1875–1926)

Who am I?

An obvious way of answering this question is by examining our
parentage and family history, the kind of enquiry pursued by the
popular TV genealogy programme, *Who Do You Think You Are?*
Normally, we can take our genetic history for granted. We can see
that in appearance we look like our father or mother, that siblings
show marked resemblances carried down the generations as
family traits. But the question takes us beyond parentage and
genetic inheritance. Who I am is also determined by environment, education and relationships.

The matter of self-identity is clearly allied to self-knowledge.
We define ourselves by what we know of ourselves, and how other
people perceive us contributes to this. While awaiting execution by
the Nazis, Dietrich Bonhoeffer (1906–1945) wrote a poem entitled,
"Who Am I?" Even in the military prison where he was confined,
Banhoeffer appeared to others to be at peace with himself –
cheerful towards his warders, and in command of his emotions.
Yet his inward self was tortured, for his own fate and that of his
friends. The poem asks if our self-knowledge reflects what other
people tell us about ourselves, or "only what I know myself". The
only certainty, since Banhoeffer was a passionate Lutheran, was
that he belonged to God.

Our name tells us nothing about who we are, it is merely a
label attached to a person: *I am David, I am Mary*, provide only
a useful point of reference. What we do is also just descriptive:
knowing that you are a shopkeeper or a doctor may indicate
some aspects of the kind of person you are because of the role

❝ *Knowing others is wisdom,*
knowing yourself is enlightenment. ❞

LAO TZU (c.570–c.490 BC)

• •

you fulfil, but it tells us nothing essential. Nor can we define who we are from the sum total of our life experience at any one time. Who am I? "I'm a Tibetan Buddhist" tells us *about* you, "I was educated in England" tells us something more, and "I'm now living in Germany" adds to the picture, but that's all we have: a picture.

To answer the question, we must consider more than just the body and its circumstances, and some would maintain that the mind and/or the soul are the key issues. This takes us into the deep waters of body/mind dualism. Are they separate entities, as René Descartes (1596–1650) proposed, or are they two very different aspects of the one being? In his *Meditation 17*, John Donne (1572–1631) famously wrote, "No man is an island, entire of itself," and what can be said with confidence is that the question "Who am I?" can only be answered in term of our relationships with others since, as Martin Buber (1878–1965) said, "in the beginning is relation": thus, "all real living is meeting."

Before I was born, was I someone else?

For Hindus and Buddhists, this is life's most meaningful question. So long-held and so profound are the ideas it raises, that we could do worse than pause to think them through.

To have lived previously and to be reborn after we die implies some kind of cycle. Buddhists have a term for this cycle of birth, death and rebirth: *samsara*, a Sanskrit word which means "journeying". To break out of the cycle of existences is to attain what is called *nirvana* – literally "extinction", or "enlightenment", which in turn brings us to an entirely different mode of being and the ultimate destination of our journey. What holds us to the cycle is acquisitiveness, our attachment to "things", and looking for fulfilment in what is merely material and transitory. This is a delusion, a mistake that affects our behaviour in every way and involves us in karma. This word means "deed", but it is as much to do with our intention as with our actions. Everything we think, do and say has a consequence: there's always a knock-on effect. Each one of us accumulates a personal karma, the sum total of our intentions, by which means we recreate ourselves. In this way we are continually evolving; and if we want to know who we were before we were born, we can obtain some indication by looking at who we are now. In the same way, if we want to know who we will be in a future existence, considering what we are thinking and doing now may give us a glimpse.

It would be unwise to see this interpretation of life's journey as a form of fatalism, a suggestion that our path is somehow definitively programmed by the consequences of our previous behaviour accumulated as karma. Karma does not seek to account for evil and suffering: it seeks to show that for every action there is a reaction, and that we have some real control over our lives. That we are beings who evolve implies the necessity of change. Such change is brought about by the choices we make.

There are, on record, accounts of people who have knowledge of a previous existence. While many seem to have been given glimpses of a previous life, most of us dwell only on the improbability of the concept. The Hindu and Buddhist traditions that gave rise to the intriguing idea of reincarnation suggest that one way of discovering who we were before we were born is to follow a meditation practice. By this means, the mind is calmed and focused in such a way as to lead us to a recovered memory of a previous lifetime.

What is self?

Usually, when we think of the idea of "self", we mean being conscious of our identity, and the qualities that make us different from others. Our self, then, might be what amounts to our uniqueness. We will be considering what this is in a later question (see page 46). Attempting to answer the question "What is self?" has been central to the work of psychologists. Freud used the term "ego", by which he meant the "I", that entity of which we are conscious that is distinct from all other aspects of the world. It is what controls thought and behaviour, our conscious awareness, our reason and common sense, all of which combine to keep us in touch with external reality. For Jung, Self is one of the archetypes

– that is, one of the innate patterns of thought acquired at birth from humanity's past collective experience. Other examples of archetypes include the Great Mother and the Hero. The Self archetype is the coherent combination of the conscious and the unconscious, which we come to know by a process Jung calls "individuation", the coming together in a unified whole of all the differentiated aspects of our makeup, or what Adler calls the "indivisibility of the personality". For Jung, this is the regulating centre of the psyche.

Philosophers have also taken up the question. Plato identified the self with the soul, Descartes with the "I" of his famous "I think, therefore I am" – that is to say, the self is what does the experiencing. However, David Hume (1711–1776) believed that what we experience are merely loose and separate "perceptions of the mind" of which our self-consciousness is but one. Immanuel Kant (1724–1804) also argued that the abiding self is the subject of ordered and coordinated experience: we have to allow a concept of self simply because "something" is doing the experiencing. In the process of experiencing, the self is susceptible to every kind of physical occurrence: it makes its own construction of the phenomenal world, which may be partly the same as that made by other "selves", or markedly different. By sensing, imagining, remembering and thinking, the self puts together its own personal mental history. As Ugo Betti (1892–1953) wrote, "When I say, 'I', I mean a thing absolutely unique, not to be confused with any other." Certainly, at the core of our consciousness, there seems to be an entity, a still point served by the term "self" – for how can something that is the subject of experience, responding to and

*❝ One may understand the cosmos,
but never the ego; the self is more distant
than any star. ❞*

G.K. CHESTERTON (1874–1936)

. . . .

assimilating constant change, be anything other than an unchanging entity?

I know by the "I" I think and speak of that I exist. I can be sure that "I am," whatever criteria I use to confirm this. That "I" is the subject of self-esteem, it has a self-image, and it likes to think of itself as being free and autonomous. We are conscious of our selves, we know what the self thinks and does, we experience self-awareness, self-doubt, self-esteem, but our problem begins when we ask what the self is – for whichever way we come at it, it seems to remain elusive.

How many selves have I got?

We are not here concerned with Multiple Personality Disorder in which the sufferer is aware of distinct, separate personalities, but with the sense many of us have that we exist, as a self, in several different ways. What we are is endlessly variable to the point where in some circumstances we might say, "I wasn't myself," or "I can't believe I actually did [or said] that." Our public self is markedly different from our private self, and we know ourselves to change according to different social environments, so that we exhibit a different self in relationship to different people. The American sociologist Charles Cooley (1864–1929) wrote of the concept of "The Looking Glass Self", suggesting that we adapt and shape ourselves to other people's opinions and perceptions of us. This is not "seeing ourselves as others see us", but *becoming* what others think we are. We do this all the time, and the constant adaptation breeds a remarkable variety of selves.

Mostly, we do this consciously. In each situation we become something different as part of the social pressure to conform, or the personal pressure to establish our uniqueness. Normally, this is not a problem, but it becomes one when in the process of not being ourselves, both we and those who know us lose sight of who we really are. People know us as a particular kind of person with all the complex aspects of character and personality that involves. But the social context constantly changes, and in our effort to be the person whom we think they know, and in response to what we think they expect us to be, we engage in self-impersonation. In each of these changing roles, be they private, social or professional, we have different desires, needs, ambitions, strengths and weaknesses.

● ●

❝ A man has as many social selves as there are individuals who recognize him. ❞

WILLIAM JAMES (1842–1910)

We also present a different self to ourselves. When we grieve, the self becomes detached as a way of easing the pain; when ashamed or hurt, the self turns inwards until we can face the problem objectively. Yet other selves are in evidence when we are happy, praised, or frightened. As we live through our kaleidoscope of experiences and the emotions they raise, one of our various selves will respond – for example, the confident self, the questioning self, the rational or intuitive self. These are, of course, all one and the same person, but different aspects of our *essential* self. The various selves fulfil different functions, and we call upon them because this is how experience has taught us how best to cope with the constant changes in our lives. The issue becomes more complicated when we consider our different areas of potential. Most people are multi-talented, but because of specific choices, often made when quite young, the full range of possibility is lost to them. The same person could successfully pursue several different careers, and each would have shaped their "selves" differently. The emerging dominant self is moulded by such choices, but the other selves remain, often to take the stage for a while. What is essential for our happiness is that we chose the path that will most fully realize the core or true self. Elisabeth Kübler-Ross (1926–2004), the Swiss psychiatrist and pioneer of "near-death" studies, pointed to the "inner self" as a priority: "It is not the end of the physical body that should worry us. Rather, our concern must be to live while we're alive – to release our inner selves from the spiritual death that comes with living behind a façade designed to conform to external definitions of who and what we are."

Can we really know ourselves?

Although a definition of self is hard to pin down, self-knowledge seems to hover at the centre of the discussion as the key to so many other aspects of knowledge. In some quarters, it is far from central. Buddhism, for example, has a radically different approach to the concept of self and self-knowledge, teaching that our sense of a personal, individual self is illusory. In contrast, the biblical religions teach a very clear concept of self, something so dominant that it serves as a barrier between ourselves and God, so that if we are to "find" God we must give up our "selves" to do so. Between these views are numerous other traditions that aim to lead their followers to know, or realize, their "true self". This essential self is hidden within a lifetime of conditioning under layers of impressions, ideas, assumptions, reasoning, philosophies, aversions, likings and discriminations. Finding our true selves, what existentialist psychologists term "self-actualization", is rather like peeling away the layers of an onion, or stripping off layers of paint to disclose the original colour. But although no literature or witness statements exist to tell us what our true self is like once it is realized, it is thought that finding our true self is indispensable to the development of our talents and potential. Certainly, our self-image considerably influences how we live our lives, but the impression we have of ourselves may differ greatly from the impression other people have of us.

On a more mundane level we need to know ourselves as completely as possible. In one sense, everything we learn contributes to self-knowledge, as Ralph Waldo Emerson (1803–1882)

❝ Self-knowledge is the property of that man whose passions have their full play, but who ponders over their results. ❞

BENJAMIN DISRAELI (1804–1881)

• •

wrote in his *Journals*: "Wherever we go, whatever we do, self is the sole subject we study and learn" – and the curriculum is considerable. The only way we can learn something new about ourselves is by seeking new experience, by journeying in what Sir Alfred Tennyson called "the untravelled world", and by taking the novelist Henry Miller's risk: "All growth is a leap in the dark, a spontaneous unpremeditated act without benefit of experience."

Can we change ourselves?

The inner, still point of ourselves, our "true self", is not going to change. In Eastern philosophy this is *atman*, the unchanging self-essence which, as we have seen, lies hidden beneath the accumulated sediment of experience and conditioning. That there is something within us that abides, that is unchanging, is reassuring, whether we think of this in temporal or eternal terms. But in other respects, the self with which we face the world is subject to inevitable and constant change. "Because things are the way they are, things will not stay as they are," as the playwright

Bertold Brecht (1898–1956) put it. The inevitability of change seems to be programmed: everything – ourselves, other people, our planet, the expanding universe – is in a state of constant flux. Many of the changes we undergo, we contrive; but, despite ourselves, we have no control over some of the influences and pressures that also change us. In both cases, there are times when we find ourselves reluctant to change, however necessary change may be.

To what extent, we can ask, am I the same person that first inhabited my body so many years ago? The American poet Ezra Pound (1885–1972) rightly said, "there is no reason why the same man should like the same book at eighteen and forty-eight." Whatever answer we give to the question, it is likely that we will have the same sense of self-identity regardless of the many ways in which we have changed. Some of these changes may be radical, such as a switch in our political or religious commitment; others

If you would attain to what you are not yet, you must always be displeased by what you are. For where you are pleased with yourself, there you have remained. Keep adding, keep walking, keep advancing.

ST AUGUSTINE (AD 354–430)

may be circumstantial, such as the death of a close relative, the termination of a marriage, or emigrating. Despite such changes, our sense of the "I" will be constant.

More subtle and perhaps more significant are changes to our character, and it is these changes that will, in the long term, be most noticeable to our friends and family, and alter our own self-image. Any of the changes mentioned above may well be due to a change in character. The extent to which we can change ourselves so as to eradicate less favourable aspects of our character, such as a criminal tendency or a disposition to alcoholism, is a question that has occupied psychologists and sociologists for a very long time. To change something embedded in our personality we would almost certainly require specialist assistance, but changing an attitude such as impatience, hypercriticism or rigidly held opinions may be dependent on the extent to which we *desire* to change, and have the will to implement this desire. A price has to be paid for any kind of change, and even though, as John Henry Newman (1801–1890) put it, "growth is the only evidence of life", that growth may be painful.

The French writer Anatole France (1844–1924) believed that life is a process of successive births and deaths: "All changes, even the most longed for, have their melancholy aspects; for what we leave behind us is part of ourselves; we must die to one life before we can enter another."

How different am I from the next man or woman?

As criminals are discovering to their cost these days, each one of us has a unique DNA, a distinctive genetic profile. Setting aside the close resemblances of twins and the similarities caused by inherited family traits, human beings represent a vast range of physical difference. More varied than physical differences are attributes of character, personality and temperament, which may constitute what it is that distinguishes us from others. We like to think that we are being ourselves most of the time, and from an early age we're encouraged to be so. There are, however, many restraints that limit the self-expression that presents to the world what being ourselves means. If we don't stand out from the crowd, what we are uniquely is probably only evident in flashes seen through the veil of familiarity through which our family and friends view us. Custom and law condition us to conform, and most younger people want to be a part of their peer group in a way that blends in, but also allows them to express what they are in distinction from others.

The American singer and actress Bette Midler (b.1945) advises, "Cherish forever what makes you unique, cuz you're really a yawn if it goes!" So, other than in physical terms, in what ways might we be different from other people? Any response would need to ignore aspects of character that are impermanent, variable and subjective – for example, attractiveness, sense of humour and aesthetic taste. With that qualification in mind, the attributes that could determine in what ways we are different from anyone else might include intelligence, cognitive ability, creative ability, temperament and introversion-extroversion. Not all of these attributes are "fixed". They do not remain entirely the same throughout a person's adult lifetime: for example, cognitive and creative ability might change according to circumstance, and none of them alone would define our personal uniqueness, but in combination they do contribute to what is called our personality.

The extent to which we are different from other people is difficult to assess. We are thrown back on the "nature versus nurture" debate for which there is no resolution, although new advances in genetics and brain science are favouring nature. It has been said that the extent to which we are unique is one of the many things we have in common, but there are those who are uncomfortable with being seen to be very different. Others, seeking ways to demonstrate their individuality, find much in society that frustrates their doing so. Rudyard Kipling (1865–1936) observed that "the individual has always had to struggle to keep from being overwhelmed by the tribe. To be your own man is a hard business. If you try it, you will be lonely often, and sometimes frightened. But no price is too high to pay for the privilege of owning yourself."

Is self-assertion always wrong?

Self-assertion is customarily associated with an aggressive promotion of self-interests, opinions and demands, in such a way as to suggest a sense of superiority to others, or of being right over and against the others' views. More positively, it can be an assertion of one's own rights and opinions against something that threatens those rights, or is believed to be morally wrong. Self-assertion can be valid if the object is to get recognition for your work or cause – if, for example, that is unjustly suppressed. As so often with matters that touch us personally, it is not what we do but how we do it that determines legitimacy, and that balance can be finely drawn. The political philosopher John Stuart Mill (1806–1873), a champion of the freedom of the individual, expressed the tension in its more extreme form: "Pagan self-assertion is one of the elements of human worth, as well as Christian self-denial."

There are three parts offered to the structural model of the psyche offered by Sigmund Freud (1856–1939): the id, the ego and the superego. The id, he wrote, "is the dark, inaccessible part of our personality ... filled with energy reaching it from the instincts. ... The ego represents what may be called reason and common sense," while the superego may be thought of as "a type of conscience that punishes misbehaviour with feelings of guilt". It is the ego that is of interest to us – that part of the psyche, to use Freud's image, that

66 The right of nature ... is the liberty each man hath to use his own power, as he will himself, for the preservation of his own nature; that is to say, of his own life. 99

THOMAS HOBBES (1588–1679)

the id rides as though it were an unruly horse that draws its energy, not from the id, but from elsewhere. While for Freud the ego was that part of the mind that held consciousness, today the word has several meanings. Philosophy has taken it to be the experienced "I", identified not with the body or the mind, but with a faculty that organizes our attitudes *towards* the body, the mind, the physical and social world. The "I" thus focuses identity and individuality and provides, like a compass, a consistent bearing by means of which we locate ourselves during our past, present and future journey through life. Self-assertion, a conscious promotion of the "I", has, with reference to the ego, become associated with self-esteem and an inflated sense of our own worth – in short, self-assertion is an expression of our egoism.

The film director Akira Kurosawa (1910–1998) distinguished sharply between egoism and altruism: "The Japanese see self-assertion as immoral, and self-sacrifice as the sensible course to take in life." What touches immorality most closely is probably selfishness, which always takes the form of self-assertion, whether blatant or covert. Oscar Wilde (1854–1900) put it in his usual pithy way: "Selfishness is not living as one wishes to live, it is asking others to live as one wishes to live." Enlightened self-interest, however, is at times essential, for it can be a survival technique, as the Babylonian Rabbi Hillel (110 BC–AD 10) understood: "If I am not for myself, who will be for me? But if I am only for myself, who am I? If not now, when?"

3
Cosmos

"We and the cosmos are one. The cosmos is a vast body, of which we are the still parts. The sun is a great heart whose tremors run through our smallest veins. The moon is a great gleaming nerve-centre from which we quiver forever."

D.H. LAWRENCE (1885–1930)

Did the universe have an origin in time?

Long before astrophysicists formulated their current theories about the origin of the universe, philosophers and theologians had tried to say something coherent on the subject. Perhaps the best-known attempts at answering this question came from religions that provided a mythical account of creation as given, for example, in Genesis. If the principle of cause and effect is applicable, the creator God represents the "First Cause" – that is, what it was that set off the whole process. In general, the Greek philosophers eschewed the concept of creation because they were suspicious of a cosmology that required divine intervention. For them, the universe and the human race had always existed and would continue to do so. For the philosopher Immanuel Kant (1724–1804) space and time originate as concepts, or constructions of the mind: we do not come by knowledge of them in the usual way, but by intuition, and our intuition is confirmed by our experience since, to use Kant's phrase, we employ both concepts to "coordinate everything sensed externally". His argument then goes on as follows: "Those, however, who assert the absolute reality of space and time, whether they take it to be subsisting or only inhering, must themselves come into conflict with the principles of experience." Kant reasoned that because time and space are "forms of sensible intuition lying ready in the mind", they constitute the context in which we learn and organize our knowledge. If the universe did not have its origin in time, this would not be possible.

However, if the universe did have a beginning in time, this

leaves open the question as to why it should have started at one particular moment. Reverting to the biblical account, St Augustine (AD354–430) did not read the Genesis story literally, describing the six days of creation as a logical framework. As he puts it in his *Sirach* (18:1), *"creavit omni simul"*: "he [God] created all things at once", and time was included in "all things".

The discovery by Edwin Hubble (1889–1953) of galaxies other than our own, based on the Doppler effect of red shift which led to the theory of the expanding universe, has taken the question out of the hands of theologians and philosophers and placed it in the hands of astrophysicists. We can no longer think of time as a dimension that exists on its own. Even if we could, the universe could not have had its origin in time in a linear sense. That is, we cannot say that at a certain point in time it began to exist. Time cannot exist independently of the universe itself, and modern theories of astrophysics are telling us that what we think of as "time" came into existence with the "Big Bang". This phrase was coined by Fred Hoyle (1915–2001) to distinguish it from his own, alternative Steady State (or Infinite Universe) theory, to be considered below. Despite its name, the "Big Bang" was not a massive explosion, but a process – again, we'll look at this shortly.

We know of time only because we also know of space. As Albert Einstein (1879–1955) demonstrated, the two combine interdependently, to give us the concept of space-time. Within this dimension, the universe did have a specific origin – that is, we know it had a beginning even if the debate about how it began, and in what way it will continue, seems as durable as the universe itself.

Is the universe infinite?

A simplistic view of the universe, once generally believed, is that it is static in the sense of being unchanging – that, like a model, it has a fixed construction. This view also holds that the unchanging universe has existed forever. This was not thought, necessarily, to be a contradiction to creationism, since it could also be believed that the universe, pretty much as we see it now, was created at a point in time – infinite in both the spatial and temporal dimensions. By a kind of magic of the pluperfect, God created a universe that had always existed.

The Big Bang Theory states that at a certain moment in time the universe came into existence by a process so enormous that it accounts for everything that is. The theory has always been popular with people who believe that, as St John put it, "no single thing" was created without God, since although the Big Bang runs contrary to, for example, the six-day account of creation in Genesis, it does allow for "something" to have taken a creative initiative. In contrast, the Infinite Universe Theory proposed in 1948 by Hoyle and others states that the universe has always existed and that it exists everywhere and has always done so. It follows that the universe will not end but will continue everlastingly. The theory allows, with a nod toward the Big Bang, that as galaxies move apart, new galaxies are formed in the expanding spaces between them from matter that is being constantly "created". Because it had no beginning, the universe is self-existing, and not the work of a creator. The idea is consistent with the First Law of Thermodynamics, which concerns the conservation of energy,

❝ The universe is then one, infinite, immobile. It is not capable of comprehension and therefore is endless and limitless, and to that extent infinite and indeterminable, and consequently immobilizable. ❞

GIORDANO BRUNO (1548–1600)

and states that "matter and the motion of matter neither can be created or destroyed." However, Stephen Hawking and Sir Roger Penrose have shown Hoyle's theory to be false, leaving the Big Bang as the standard cosmological model. What the 1978 Nobel prize winners Arno Penzias and Robert Wilson found that denied the Hoyle view of the cosmos was cosmic microwave background radiation (CMBR). Radio telescopes have shown that the spaces between stars are not, as once thought, pitch-black but glow uniformly, and most strongly in the radio spectrum associated with microwaves. The "glow" is just there, it has no present source, and is evidence of earlier phases of the expansion and cooling of the universe, thus corroborating the theory of the Big Bang and the subsequent cosmic expansion. Hawking has gone on more recently to espouse M-theory, which appears to prepare the way for an infinite *number* of universes: "Quantum fluctuations," he has said, "lead to the spontaneous creation of tiny universes, out of nothing. Most of the universes collapse to nothing, but a few that reach a critical size, will expand in an inflationary manner, and will form galaxies and stars, and maybe beings like us."

This takes us into a realm of science where it is easy for the lay reader to feel lost, as in a hall of intellectual mirrors. We sense that we are reading about abstractions rather than empirical reality. It is difficult, in any case, to transcend the limits of what the humanities-trained intellect can comprehend. Unable to give concrete imaginative form to edgelessness, we fall back on a commonsense extrapolation – from our perception of the enormity of what we can see above us with the naked eye or, even more thrillingly, through binoculars or a telescope.

However, extraordinary as this may seem, modern astrophysics is tending toward the notion that our universe is finite. This confronts us with a paradox, that while the universe is not infinite in space, nor does space have any boundary, it is, as Einstein demonstrated, curved. Hawking provides us with a dizzying summary: "when one combines general relativity with the uncertainty principle of quantum mechanics, it is possible for both space and time to be finite without edges or boundaries."

Most of us have to contemplate such enigmas with our feet firmly planted on Earth. Finite or infinite, the universe exists in space, which is imaginable only as a vague and measureless wilderness, stretching as far as the mind can imagine – but starting, at least, near home. As Fred Hoyle comfortingly reminds us, space "isn't remote at all. It's only an hour's drive away if your car could go straight upwards."

Did time have a beginning and will it have an end?

Before the Big Bang, all the matter in the universe would have been in one place, a state known as a singularity, exhibiting infinite density and temperature. Rather than the explosion suggested by the phrase "Big Bang", what happened was an expansion of the singularity. The "Big Bang" was whatever set the expansion process in motion, re-forming the infinite density and the infinitesimal volume as the universe we now observe, and so originating space and time. Before this happened, none of the laws of physics we now know, such as gravity and thermodynamics, would have been in operation; but once the process got underway, all physical laws would have been activated. The Second Law of Thermodynamics concerns the principle of decay, and because the process of decay accelerates with time, the universe will, one day, collapse, bringing time to an end.

Stephen Hawking (b.1942), in his *A Brief History of Time,* proposed what he called the three arrows of time. His account of these contributes to our understanding of what time is, and how it works; it also moves us from a concept of time as a construction of mind, to a concept that combines physical law, psychology and cosmology. The direction of the first arrow is determined by the Second Law of Thermodynamics, the speed at which disorder or entropy increases. Second is the psychological arrow of time – that is, the way we feel or sense time passing, our consciousness of the present, our memories of things past. Thirdly, we have the cosmological arrow of time, determined by the direction in which the universe is expanding. Only when all three arrows point in the same direction do conditions prevail for the development of a life-form intelligent enough to ask questions. However, Professor Hawking tells us that quantum theory "introduces a new idea, that of imaginary time," which although it sounds like science fiction is, "nevertheless, a genuine scientific concept." If we imagine that time is like one of these lines of print, the past will be on the left, and the future on the right, but imaginary time assumes another vertical direction. It is imaginary "because it is not the kind of time we normally experience. But in a sense, it is just as real as what we call real time." So we have time defined by the directions of the three arrows, and the direction of imaginary time; and all four of these are contained within the physical universe, and therefore have both a beginning and an end.

While Western philosophy is dominated by a linear concept of time, there are peoples, such as the Maya, who hold time to be circular. The idea is based on the time periods that the heavenly bodies take to complete their cycles, be it a lunar month or the far longer, 26,000-year period of precession which returns Earth and the stars to a particular alignment. The recurring cyclic patterns of nature seem to lend credence to the concept, but whether repeated periods of time also imply repetitions of history remains an open question. Shelley believed it did: "history is a cyclic poem written by time upon the memories of man." Time, as Stephen Hawking assures us, had a beginning and will have an end. "The conclusion of this lecture is that the universe has not existed forever. Rather, the universe, and time itself, had a beginning in the Big Bang, about 15 billion years ago," and he goes on to add that "even if the universe does come to an end, it won't be for at least twenty billion years." Hawking has calculated that the beginning of the universe occurred between 13.3 and 13.9 billion years ago.

Does our planet have a future?

As we have seen, the universe is likely to continue for at least 20 billion years, a period impossible to imagine. The end, when it comes, will be a collapse, but we've little idea of what form this collapse will take. However, this says nothing about the potential life of our own solar system sustained by our own sun. It is theoretically possible that the solar system could collapse before the universe does, an event that might be symptomatic of a greater malaise.

The sun was formed only 4.57 billion years ago, against the universe's formation by the Big Bang 13.3 to 13.9 billion years ago. The sun is halfway through what is termed its main-sequence

Unless we wish to perish, we must shake off our old prejudices and build the Earth. The more scientifically I regard the world, the less can I see any possible biological future for it except in the active consciousness of its unity.

PIERRE TEILHARD DE CHARDIN (1881–1955)

evolution, which, it is estimated, will last for another 10 billion years; but in about 5 billion years it will enter the red giant phase, risking the existence of the Earth, which might be consumed by the sun. But in only one billion years, the surface of the Earth will be too hot to hold water; and, thus, life on Earth will cease.

If we respond to the question of the future of planet Earth in terms of the span of human life rather than universal life, we are directed to matters such as ecology and the projected increase in population. Undoubtedly, life on Earth will change radically over time. More and more species of animals and plants will become extinct, the extremes of weather will become more marked, the problems of housing and feeding people, more urgent.

Current interest in the Mayan prophecies, together with Chinese astrological predictions, suggest that the Earth faces extinction as early as 2012. Calendar predictions apart, it is thought by some that our planet is imminently at risk from sun storms, asteroid impact, an accident involving the European particle accelerator, the eruption of a super volcano, or changes in the Earth's magnetic field.

These are distinct possibilities and they are currently being monitored by agencies such as NASA, the Armagh Observatory in Ireland and the Centre of Astrobiology at Cardiff University. No one can know when such an event might take place. Douglas Adams (1952–2001) provides a more realistic and responsible scenario: "We don't have to save the world. The world is big enough to look after itself. What we have to be concerned about is whether or not the world we live in will be capable of sustaining us in it."

Whose universe is this?

A BBC 2 *Horizon* programme, broadcast in April 2007, told the story of a Nevada entrepreneur, Dennis Hope, who had found a loophole in the 1967 UN Outer Space Treaty, and claimed ownership of the Earth's moon, together with seven planets and their moons. Mr Hope maintained that these are "truly unowned lands. We're doing exactly what our forefathers did when they came to the New World from the European continent." Corporations, Hollywood stars, hotel chains and three former US Presidents are among those who have bought lunar real estate from him, and by 2007 he'd amassed 9 million dollars. It is believed that China and Russia are also considering staking their claim to property in space. Inevitably, this is a commercial initiative, because there are potentially huge profits to be made from surface-mining the moon to extract a rare gas, helium 3, which is a source of clean, pollution-free energy.

There are numerous internet agencies that offer to sell you a star, or invite you, at a price, to name a star you subsequently "own". This is a scam. The International Planetarium Society's guidelines on star naming make the rules clear: "The star names recognised and used by scientists are those that have been published by astronomers at credible scientific institutions. The International Astronomical Union, the worldwide federation of astronomical societies, accepts and uses only those names. Such names are never sold."

With regard to actual ownership and occupation, it can only be hoped that there will be an international agreement similar to that for the Arctic and Antarctic, which allows occupation only for purposes of research. But celestial real estate apart, the question remains, whose universe is it?

For the greater part of our history, the universe was thought to have been the realm of the gods, some associated with specific planets – for example the god of war with Mars and the goddess of love with Venus. The gods, it seemed, populated the heavens like stars populate Hollywood. It was given to the Jews to provide us with an account of creation that made the one God responsible for everything, an account equally authoritative for Christians and Muslims. It followed that God, as creator, was also the proprietor of the universe. For Hindus and Buddhists the matter scarcely arises, firstly because all phenomena are believed to be constructs of the mind, and secondly because it is understood that over extremely long periods of time the visible universe declines and dies, only to re-evolve. Perhaps we should note that the kinds of questions we have so far been considering are among the fourteen unanswerable questions the Buddha remained silent about. Such speculations, he taught, cause "fever, unease, bewilderment and suffering". In our contemplation of the universe, there will be those agreeing with the Buddha who might well add the current question to his list.

Michel de Montaigne (1533–1592) made a good point: "The finest thing in the world is knowing how to belong to oneself". Only then can we make the universe our own.

Is it possible for us to feel "at home" in the universe?

For some people, the universe is either a vast and threatening place, or something that is "just there", occasionally acknowledged by a glance at the sky, but otherwise irrelevant. Because our minds are finite, and our lifespan is measured by a blink of the cosmic eye, it is not surprising that we find the idea of an infinite universe that has always been there, alienating. We can sympathize with Blaise Pascal (1623–1662) when he says, "the eternal silence of infinite space frightens me." Even if we could bring to our understanding of the universe the insights of modern astrophysics, many, like Stephen Weinberg, would find that "the more the universe seems comprehensible, the more it also seems pointless." If we cannot find a purpose in the universe, how can we find a purpose for ourselves?

Traditionally, only by resorting to religion have people felt at home in the universe, a place vaguely associated with heaven, our eternal destination. Having faith that the universe was created by a beneficent God, and that they too were part of that creation, had the effect, for "believers", of giving both creation and human life a

. . . .

* The soul knows no home in the modern cosmos.* **”**

RICHARD TARNAS (B.1950)

purpose. The Anthroposophist Rudolph Steiner (1861–1925) taught that we are intimately bound up with the whole cosmos, even to the physical structure of our bodies, and that the way to feel at home in the universe is to understand our unique significance. In his Introduction to Steiner's book *At Home in the Universe,* Paul Margulies writes: "The Earth is not our home. Our true home is in the world of stars. ... Without some sense that we are spiritual beings we feel neither at home in the world of stars nor here on Earth."

Is religious faith, then, a condition of our feeling at home in the universe? The American physicist David Bohm (1917–1992) made the point that "in some sense man is a microcosm of the universe; therefore what man is, is a clue to the universe. We are enfolded in the universe." Experiencing this "enfolding" is not dependent on religious belief. Many experience the universe aesthetically from what can be observed of it, most of us gathering an increasing sense of awe and wonder the more science reveals to us of its origin and nature. Like Wordsworth, we can acquire

> A sense of the sublime,
> Of something far more deeply interfused,
> Whose dwelling is the light of setting suns,
> And the round ocean and the living air,
> And the blue sky, and in the mind of man.

We are thrown back, it seems, on our awareness of everything, especially self-awareness and self-knowledge: the more we know, understand and feel at ease with ourselves, the more we will feel ourselves to be, naturally, a part of the whole.

Does it matter if we are alone in the universe?

A 16th-century Italian monk, Giordano Bruno (1548–1600), a philosopher, mathematician and astronomer, wrote, "In space there are numberless earths circling around other suns, which may bear upon themselves creatures similar or even superior to those upon our human Earth." Unsurprisingly, he was burned at the stake in 1600. In 1900, the French Academy of Science offered the Guzman prize of 100,000 francs "to the person of whatever nation who will find the means within the next ten years of communicating with a star and receiving a response". Mars was excluded, because at that time it was believed to be inhabited and, thus, communication with it would be too easy. The origin of life, and whether life exists anywhere else, remain beguiling questions, and only relatively recently has the subject of extraterrestrial beings moved from science fiction to science. A NASA article, "Life in the Cosmos", has this to say: "The search for life beyond our planet of origin is one of the most compelling quests in science. Are we alone in the Universe? Or is the Universe, like our planet, crowded with a variety of life that will challenge humanity's understanding of itself?" Evidence of oceans of liquid water has been discovered beneath the frozen surface of Europa, a large satellite of Jupiter, but Mars seems to remain the best place to look for extraterrestrial life, since evidence of water there suggests that its geology and environment had a similar history to Earth. In 1996, NASA announced that a meteorite that had landed on Earth 13,000 years ago in Antarctica, recovered in 1984, contained microfossils of Martian bugs. There is now no expectancy of finding life within our own solar system, but that there are millions of solar systems besides our own makes intriguingly plausible the possibility that a planet in orbit around another sun may support some form of life.

Western philosophy and religious doctrine have conditioned us to believe that life on Earth, with all its biodiversity, is unique; and, further, that the human species is alone in the cosmos in having imagination, combined with moral responsibilities and the potential for an enlightened spirit or soul. That sense of being alone has fostered our self-image and has confirmed what the various creation mythologies have indicated, that we are superior to all other forms of life. The possibility of life elsewhere expands the territory of our global village to unimaginable horizons, especially if that life is intelligent. That we have not yet received a signal indicating the presence of life on another planet within the cosmos does not mean that no such life exists. If such a signal were received, or extraterrestrial life encountered in another way,

In space there are numberless earths circling around other suns, which may bear upon them creatures similar or even superior to those upon our human Earth.

GIORDANO BRUNO (1548–1600)

it would be hugely significant, not least for the fresh questions many would ask about the purpose of our life on Earth, and the possibility of non-human souls. As Sir Martin Rees, the Astronomer Royal (b.1942), put it, "our cosmos would seem far more interesting; we would look at a distant star with renewed interest if we knew it was another Sun, shining on a world as intricate and complex as our own."

4
Humankind

" *I do not value any view of the universe into which man and the institutions of man enter very largely and absorb much of the attention. Man is but the place where I stand, and the prospect hence is infinite.* "

HENRY DAVID THOREAU (1817–1862)

Is a human being just another animal?

Certain it is that we are animals of the genus *Homo*, although only relatively recently did Darwin demonstrate that primates are our evolutionary ancestors. It has been calculated by scientists that we separated from a common ancestry with chimpanzees between 5 and 7 million years ago. Some of our more immediate ancestors, such as *Homo erectus* and *Homo sapiens neanderthalensis*, are now extinct, while our own "out of Africa" species began to migrate across Europe 50,000 to 100,000 years ago. These are the bare bones of a complicated process for which, in terms of location and migration, there are alternative theories.

The biblical religions marked out humanity as set apart, the unique crowning glory of God's "point in time" creation, but evolution, as the "Scientific Revolution", pointed to a very long process that blurred the creationist distinctions between ourselves and other animals. We learned that we were made in the image of a higher primate, rather than God – that, as Richard Tarnas put it, "the human mind was not a divine endowment but a biological tool". Humankind, like all other species, is subject to natural selection – a process developed and sustained by natural law.

Current research (for example, R.J. Britten, *Proceedings of the National Academy of Science,* 2002) says that the similarity of our DNA with chimpanzees is about 95 per cent. Humans have 23 pairs of chromosomes, while chimpanzees have 24. While allowing that we are biologically only marginally different from chimps, there are clear distinctions to be made between ourselves and them, and although we remain animals, the differences give

❝ What a piece of work is man ... ❞

WILLIAM SHAKESPEARE (1564–1616), FROM *HAMLET*

. . . .

rise to a radically different way of, and perception of, life. Most notable, perhaps, is that we live with a sense of our own mortality, which alone provides a unique framework for existence. We can reflect on this, and every other aspect of our lives; we can develop philosophies to further our understanding; we have sophisticated languages and electronic means of communication; we can survive in elements that are alien to us; we can swim, walk and run, fly people around the world and to the moon; we are creative across an extraordinary range of disciplines; we can both prevent and create life, alter its forms, make aesthetic judgments and are potentially capable of destroying life on Earth.

Hamlet marvelled at our being "infinite in faculties", and it is these that define our differences from other animals, although Hamlet was unable to see the evolutionary process behind them. But we are not by any means the most beneficent or friendly beast to have walked the planet, and the jury is still out on how valid is Hamlet's assessment of us as "the paragon of animals".

What is death?

Whether of ourselves or others, we can never experience death, only dying. Death, as the termination of life, is the state of being dead, it is the cessation of the biological functions that define an organism, and by which we can tell if it is living. What death is, is therefore dependent on how life is defined, and there is no agreement on this. If we say that death is the cessation of vital bodily functions, we are thrown back on what these are, but conventionally the absence of life is indicated by there being no spontaneous respiratory and cardiac functions. Both of these can be artificially sustained, however, at which point the issue becomes one of how long life can be supported in this way before it is clear that there will be no improvement in the conditions threatening these functions. The term "brain death" was first used in the UK in 1976 to distinguish between patients who have a functional capacity to recover, at least partially, and those who have no chance at all. A patient deemed to be "brainstem dead" is one who will definitely not recover, not one who is already dead.

It has been suggested that the purpose of life is to learn how to die. It's a sombre agenda, and although we live with the knowledge of our mortality, we can't, all the time, consciously pass through life as though walking through "the valley of the shadow of death". Most of the world's major religions encourage their followers to keep their eye on the distant horizon of death,

Death is the supreme festival on the road to freedom.

DIETRICH BONHOEFFER (1906–1945)

not wondering when they will die but, as Brother David Steindl-Rast, the Roman Catholic theologian (b.1926), expressed it, in order to see "every moment of life as a challenge to incorporate that awareness of dying into every moment, so as to become more fully alive".

There are many accounts of what is termed a "near-death experience", which seems to be the only way in which death can actually be experienced. Either the subject approaches the death state so closely as to be able to provide a description of it or, in some rarer cases, has been pronounced dead only to "return" to bear witness to the experience. In the latter case, we might say the experience is one of a temporary transcendence of death. Near-death experiences have been researched by university medical, psychiatric and psychology faculties, and have been shown to have certain characteristics in common, including the awareness of having been dead. Other "sensations" described are a sense of peace; of being outside the world or outside the body; of passing through a tunnel; of rapid movement toward, then emergence into, a light with which it's possible to communicate; an overwhelming sense of love; a meeting with spiritual beings, themselves blazing or glowing with light or else dressed in white; the approach to some kind of border; a review of your life; the sense of knowing or understanding the nature of the universe; a connection to your own religious or spiritual culture; and a decision as to whether or not you return to your body. (The foregoing is a summary of features of near-death experiences given in books included in Further Reading, page 206.)

From these accounts, it would seem that we can be conscious

of being taken very close to death. Whether our consciousness can survive the actual death of the physical body is a subject taken up by other questions in this book.

Is there life after death?

Setting aside questions of faith, nothing can be said with certainty about life continuing after death, and only atheists seem able to give a confident answer – which is negative, of course. Almost from the beginnings of human society, belief in life after death has been built into our culture. That we can survive death is one of the central teachings of biblical religion, and we can be sure that this belief was present in the traditions from which they originated. The way in which we survive death is pictured differently among the major world faiths: Judaism has a generalized drawn concept of *Olam Ha-Ba*, "the world to come", where the righteous will enjoy an afterlife. Across its different denominations Christianity carries various images of the heaven that awaits the righteous. These include Paradise (as an Eden-like garden) and the Kingdom of God (or Kingdom of Heaven). The latter may be either "otherworldly" or an actual regime on Earth enjoyed by the resurrected and ruled over by Jesus Christ. The Qur'an (Surah Ar-Rad) also speaks of an afterlife in Eden: "The parable of the Garden which the righteous are promised" (13:35). Hinduism holds to the rebirth and reincarnation of the imperishable "soul", a process determined by one's karma, or deeds; its ultimate goal is not some form of heaven, but liberation. In Buddhism, reincarnation usually means transmigration; life is passed on like a flame lighting one candle after another, each

❝ As long as you are not aware of the continual law of Die and Be Again, you are merely a vague guest on a dark Earth. ❞

JOHANN WOLFGANG VON GOETHE (1749–1832)

flame being causally connected with, yet not the same as, its predecessor. *nirvana* is the state of final liberation from this process, extinguishing the candle flame. Once free of the cycle of birth, death and rebirth, individual consciousness is absorbed into the whole. When asked for greater clarity on this process, the Buddha said it was "incomprehensible, indescribable, inconceivable, unutterable". This is the Buddha's way of saying that the subject is a mystery, like that of creation and the origin of the universe – as there are no clear answers, we should not dwell on the matter unduly.

Despite the influence on our culture of the concept of the resurrection of the body, there are few who believe that we will, one day, physically survive death – that, miraculously, our decayed or cremated forms will be reconstituted. If there is some form of survival, it will be spiritual – a soul, perhaps, that retains an element of consciousness. Opposed to such a belief are the opinions of atheists, notably the evolutionary biologist Richard Dawkins (b.1941), author of many excellent books, most recently the controversial *The God Delusion*. Such people maintain that since there is no scientific evidence for a life after death, the concept can, at best, only be a myth sustained by faith. Dawkins tells us, "faith is the great cop-out, the great excuse to evade the need to think and evaluate evidence. Faith is belief in spite of, even perhaps because of, the lack of evidence." By believing that we can survive death, we cushion ourselves against the stark, cold truth of death being truly terminal, and everything ceasing. An alternative perception is that of Albert Schweitzer (1875–1965): "Reincarnation contains a most comforting explanation of reality by means of which Indian thought surmounts difficulties which baffle the thinkers of Europe." As well as being comforting, it is also, I would argue, intellectually the most satisfactory answer to the question, Are we born only to die?

Does life have a purpose?

The meaning and purpose of our lives are tied up with the meaning and purpose of the universe. Since we are part of the whole and subject to the same physical laws as the endless galaxies, it is unlikely that our lives will have a purpose independently of everything else. For the inanimate, material world, purpose can be construed as conformity to the principles of physics, to being a functional part of the working harmony of the whole. Such purpose is derived from natural laws, but it may be that "purpose" is not quite the best word to describe their function. For humankind, purpose is allied to consciousness. When we consider the meaning of our lives, we do so knowing that the physical laws of our universal environment determine our parameters, and that within this cosmic context our own genetic code defines further limits. No one had the purpose of being born, we had no control over our being here, life is an event thrust upon us, and we can either live our lives as if they were meaningless, or find in life, or bring to it, a sense of purpose.

According to religion, life's main purpose is the cultivation of a close relationship with God, or the divine. Most religions teach that there are barriers to that union, be it the biblical religions' emphasis on sin, or the ignorance and illusion of which Eastern traditions warn. These barriers are to be overcome, and the means offered for achieving this give life its driving purpose. But there is another item on the agenda, of equal importance, and that is life's moral dimension – the "call" to live life according to certain ethical standards so as to hold our place on the moral high ground. We are encouraged to live for others as well as for ourselves, and altruism, whether inspired by a religious or secular mandate, has always provided life with a purpose. Many other factors may

. . . .

Our minds are finite, and yet even in these circumstances of finitude we are surrounded by possibilities that are infinite, and the purpose of life is to grasp as much as we can out of that infinitude.

ALFRED NORTH WHITEHEAD (1861–1947)

contribute to giving us a purpose in life, not the least that we don't look to life *for* a purpose, but that we *bring* a purpose to life. We don't, then, ask, what on Earth am I doing here, but what can I best do while I am here? As a Chinese proverb puts it, "the miracle is not to fly in the air, or to walk on the water, but to walk on the earth." Where and how we do this is mostly in our own hands. Some would say that we are here to get to know and understand ourselves and others, to make a contribution to bettering this world during the short time we have it. We either work to live, or live to work. And there are also those who strive to be happy, living a kind of hedonism bent on filling the gaps between eating and sleeping in the most interesting or pleasurable way. We're born, we die, but as the Jewish proverb has it, in between a bite of food and a drink come in handy.

The French philosopher Albert Camus (1913–1960) warned that "You will never live if you are looking for the meaning of life." Perhaps this is one instance when an excessive preoccupation with the question confuses the answer? Even so, Nietzsche is probably right in suggesting that if we know why we live, we'll never have a problem about *how* to live.

Can we ever be truly happy?

Happiness is a state of mind determined by attitudes, disposition and temperament. No one person's happiness can be the same as another's, but each person's happiness can contribute to someone else's, just as it can be diminished by their unhappiness. It is possible that we can be truly happy for a while, but doubtful that

❝ Happiness is the meaning and the purpose of life, the whole aim and end of human existence. ❞

ARISTOTLE (384–322 BC)

we can be lastingly happy, since even with the most positive attitude, few can surmount every change of circumstance that undermines our disposition for happiness.

What makes someone truly happy is usually personal and subjective. Some people are consistently happy regardless of their circumstances, while others enjoy only fleeting moments of happiness. However, there seem to be some common features in the conditions of happiness. The consistently happy are likely to be disposed to happiness, not prone to anxiety; they will be optimistic and positive, living fully in the present moment, relying not only on reason and intelligence, but also on intuition; they will be wise enough to know that things can change, so setbacks will not take them by surprise; and when life does becomes difficult, they will be resilient. Happiness will come more easily to those who are not too materialistic or acquisitive, but are content to make a living to meet their basic needs. Their family and friends will be important to them, and life's purpose will often be related to their careers.

For many, happiness is derived from religious faith. However difficult life may be, believing themselves to be supported by the strength and compassion of their God, such people will sustain inner peace. Others derive similar strength from quiet reflection, their happiness founded on the independence referred to in the Hindu text *Manusmriti (The Laws of Manu):* "Depend not on another, but lean instead on thyself. True happiness is born of self-reliance."

Clearly, we cannot always be happy. There will be times when we will have reason to be sad, angry, disappointed, frustrated, unwell, responding negatively to everything and everyone. Some will bounce back quickly, others will need more time. We may be happier if we take recourse to three simple measures: firstly, smiling more, since smiling, whether or not we *feel* happy, can elevate our mood; secondly, cultivating a sense of gratitude for who we are and what we have; thirdly, by finding something helpful to do, possibly for someone less happy than ourselves. In his 1693 *Essay Concerning Human Understanding,* the English philosopher John Locke (1632–1704) wrote that "the highest perfection of intellectual nature lies in a careful and constant pursuit of true and solid happiness," a thought echoed by the United States Declaration of Independence, which listed among the inalienable or sovereign rights of man, "life, liberty and the pursuit of happiness".

Can hope be a dangerous delusion?

"But what is Hope?" asked Lord Byron (1788–1824) rhetorically. "Nothing but the paint on the face of Existence. The least touch of truth rubs it off, and then we see what a hollow-cheeked harlot we have got hold of."

Notwithstanding Byron's scepticism, for many hope is the belief that there will be a positive conclusion to whatever short- or long-term projects we are engaged with, especially when that conclusion is threatened and made difficult to achieve. Stemming from an optimistic disposition, hope is a state of mind that also engenders a feeling of promise and well-being. It is the positive attitude threaded into the fabric of our personality. However strong our hope, it can be touched with anxiety and the need to assess the likelihood of the outcome. Paul's first letter to the Corinthians famously highlights "hope" as one of the most important and lasting human qualities: "But now abideth faith, hope, love, these three; and the greatest of these is love."

Unrealistic hope, however, can be a dangerous delusion, as can misplaced faith, and certain forms of love. Like faith and love, hope functions at its best only with a certain degree of maturity, when we've accumulated enough of life's experiences to enable us to judge when hope is misplaced. Although Theocritus (3rd century BC) tells us that "while there's life there's hope, and only the dead have none," some situations will appear to be completely hopeless. A person diagnosed with an inoperable terminal disease is not likely to hope for a long life and would be unwise to do so. In such circumstances, hope, Aristotle wrote, "is a waking dream". And yet, sometimes, faced with impossible circumstances, such as those that threaten life, to hope is the only thing we can do. The extraordinary accounts of the survival of Shackleton's Antarctic expedition provide an example of the extent to which survival can be dependent on the strength of a person's hope. There are dozens of similar stories of people surviving against the odds on mountains, at sea or caught up with natural disasters such as floods or earthquakes. But the point has to be made that, in every case, no one has survived on hope alone. Whatever the circumstances, hope, at its best, is allied to the will, the determination to realize what is hoped for, and hope allied to will can never be passive; together they bring about the actions needed to bring about the realization of the hope.

There are times too, of course, when we hope simply because we lack sufficient knowledge, or because what may happen in the future is a matter of speculation. We hope that our good health, and that of our family and friends, will be sustained, we hope that our livelihood will remain secure, we hope that the problems of the Middle East will be resolved, we hope that the threats to our planet's ecology will be addressed, and so on. Such hopes can only be sustained when we are sure that appropriate measures are being taken – steps to address the circumstances that threaten our health or our finances, or the peace process or the campaign to cut carbon emissions. The novelist Alexandre Dumas (1802–1870) wrote about a long-suffering Count, who combined hope with patience. Wrongly incarcerated in his dungeon, he came to understand that "until the day when God will deign to reveal the future to man, all human wisdom is contained in these two words: Wait and hope."

Do we have free will?

❝ Everything in nature is the result of fixed laws. ❞

CHARLES DARWIN (1809–1882)

. . . .

This question is usually discussed in opposition to the idea of determinism. Free will assumes that we choose and act according to our own voluntary decisions, subject to influence but free of absolute causation. The determinist view is that all events, including those of our own lives, are predetermined by a permutation of factors completely outside our control. The notion of determinism is taken up by those religions established around a creator God, who being omnipotent preordains everything that will happen. Such a view has problems, even for religious people, since most faiths hold us responsible for our deeds, which, if predetermined, cannot be said to be our responsibility. Determinism also provides a built-in excuse for even the worst of bad behaviour, since it can be argued that the subject couldn't help what he or she was doing: as doing it was predestined. People are, generally, reluctant to let go of the idea that their choices and actions derive from anything other than their own free will. They feel that the determinist alternative makes them puppets to some divine or celestial string-puller. Nor are we at ease with the idea that we are robots constructed with enormous complexity but programmed and controlled from a fingerboard held in the hands of a cosmic despot.

The argument for biological and cosmological determinism is led by evolutionary biologists and physicists. Richard Dawkins (b.1941), for example, has written of "the selfish gene", the molecules that "enslave" us. All that matters is their staying power, and to that end our bodies and minds "are their survival machines", and our behaviour is determined by them. Einstein also believed that everything is determined: "we all dance to a mysterious tune, intoned in the distance by an invisible piper."

But such programming, as irrefutable as it seems, does not tell the entire story. As with many such questions asked within the context of scientific absolutism, the matter of free will can be argued relatively. It can be maintained that our DNA necessarily programs us to exercise free will within a wide frame of reference. It becomes merely a word game to say, for example, that if we change our minds about something, it has been determined that we should do so. No one can doubt that our appearance, personality and disposition are fashioned by our genetic code, but our relationships, our education and environment, the way that from birth we absorb and use our accumulated knowledge and experience, provide a matrix so complex as to make our exercise of free will sufficiently real that any qualification is meaningless. Perhaps the distinction made by Arthur Schopenhauer (1788–1860) is closer to the truth: "A man can surely do what he wills to do, but cannot determine what he wills."

What is mind?

"Mind" is one of those words, like "good", "soul" and "beauty", that have carried a wide range of different meanings since the Greek philosophers first considered them. For the early philosophers, *nous,* the Greek for "mind", meant knowledge and reason, for Plato (*c.*428–*c.*348 BC) the rational part of the soul, for Aristotle (384–322 BC) the active and passive aspects of the intellect – Plato's version being immortal and eternal. The mind cannot, usefully, be examined on its own, and Western philosophy has always focused on how it is related to the body – that is, whether or not the mind can function and exist independently of the body and therefore is, or carries, that aspect of a person that might survive death. Whatever this relationship might be, mind is associated with thinking: it is the "place" where we receive and process our experience.

For René Descartes (1596–1650), the irreducible essence of a person was consciousness, for which thinking was the evidence. This consciousness was the only certainty expressed in his famous phrase, "I think, therefore I am." While Descartes recognized "thinking" as the essence of human life, he also recognized material objects, which don't think for themselves; nor does our thinking about them confirm their existence. Descartes' distinction between the thinking entity and "stuff" gave rise to what has become known as Cartesian dualism. Subsequently, most other philosophers sought to find solutions to this seemingly irreconcilable distinction. Baruch Spinoza (1632–1677), for example, argued that the mental and physical are simply two aspects of the same underlying reality. Eastern religions, although working from different premises, take the overcoming of dualism as their central quest, seeing our consciousness of the world as an illusion, thus making discrimination pointless.

The relationship between mind and body is also a central concern for psychologists, for whom the mind is the means by which we experience, perceive and communicate; and since we can't get outside our minds, it is the only means we have. For psychologists, the mind is a hugely complex machine, the source of all thought and behaviour. Mind can be thought of as the sum total of all the brain's activities, and as such it has no specific location within the brain. That the mind remains elusive is demonstrated by the way in which psychologists work from the outside in: they start with human behaviour, the only observable data available, and from these observations they deduce how the mind *works*, rather than what it is. From the way we behave they can "observe" our emotions and memories, our perceptions, dreams, desires,

" What we call a mind is nothing but a heap or collection of different perceptions, united together by certain relations and supposed, though falsely, to be endowed with a perfect simplicity and identity. "

DAVID HUME (1711–1776)

beliefs, ambitions, and values. Such observations and deductions are the raw materials of what is thought of as "the science of the mind".

We hear much about "strength of mind", in reference to our will and resolution. Our "state" of mind can make us ill, it can also return us to health, and it can determine failure or success. As the poet John Milton (1608–1674) put it, "the mind is its own place, and itself, can make a heaven of Hell, a hell of Heaven".

Can we know our own mind?

We spend the greater part of our lives mind-reading the minds of others. From their behaviour, facial expressions, what they say, how they live, we pick up signals that we interpret in terms of their feelings, opinions, beliefs and so on. The closer the relationship, the more likely our mind reading will be on the mark. Some people are close enough in a particular relationship to claim to know what the other is thinking: this may be intuitive, or more rarely a form of mind reading known as mental telepathy.

Can we read or know our own minds, and if so, how do we do it? The question runs parallel to an earlier one about self-knowledge. "Know thyself" was famously inscribed on a temple at Delphi. The recommendation was taken up by Alexander Pope (1688–1744): "Know then thyself, presume not God to scan. The proper study of Mankind is Man." It would be pedantic to try and draw too sharp a distinction between knowing ourselves and knowing our own minds. Mind can be understood as an aspect of self, the absolute centre of what we are. Socrates (469–399 BC), for whom mind was soul, would have us look especially "at that part of the soul in which virtue resides". Contemplating our potential for doing good, he suggests, would help us to know the true nature of our minds. In other words, to know our own minds, we need to know not just what we think, but how we think. Knowing our disposition to think in certain ways will illuminate the mind we're trying to know.

Usually, when we speak of someone knowing their own mind, we think of their ability to make decisions – it's a matter of the incisiveness or hesitancy of their decision-making and also the correctness of their choice. But there is more to it than that. The mind, as we have seen, is a tool, and no two minds are alike. Our mind is our own, and it's best that we keep it that way. Knowing our own mind as a tool means knowing what it can best do, its special qualities, and what impairs it from functioning well. Knowing our own minds means having some notion of the sharpness of our intelligence, a concept we will consider below. Seen in this way, not only can we know our own mind, but it's important for us to do so, since our mind is the tool by which we fashion everything we do. We may discover that we have a sharp or a muddled mind, a conceptual or non-conceptual mind, a mathematical or intuitive mind, an alert or impaired mind. Whatever kind of mind we discover we have, Jiddu Krishnamurti (1895–1986) writes that, "very few sustain or maintain the quality of a mind that is young … a mind that is uncontaminated by the accidents or incidents of life … a young mind is always deciding anew."

Is intelligence overrated?

What intelligence is and how it works remains something of a mystery, and the debates that it stimulates are usually controversial. Generally, the term refers to our ability to acquire knowledge and apply skills, but this broad definition has been narrowed to focus on what we might term the "intellect". The intellect is usually explained as our ability to reason: it is our objective, as opposed to our subjective, understanding and thus it is our mental ability. The faculty of intellect is thought to be the cutting edge of our intelligence, and it follows that an intelligent person is a clever person. However, there is more to be said.

Intelligence is tested with a view to assessing the extent or amount of the subject's brain power – that is, whether the person's Intelligence Quotient (IQ) registers as low / high on a scale built into the test. One of the more familiar tests is that offered by Mensa, a society formed to assess and bring together people of high intelligence. The problem with such tests is that they cannot claim to be scientific. It is not possible to prevent the results from being compromised by the mood or attitudes of the subject, and the possibility that the nature of the test is simply not appropriate for the way the

❝ Man becomes *man only by his intelligence, but he* is *man only by his heart. ❞*

HENRI-FRÉDÉRIC AMIEL (1821–1881)

subject thinks and perceives. It is, nevertheless, accepted as being a useful indicator of a person's mental abilities. More problematic is the way in which such tests are used – for example, when their purpose is to create an "élite" among children, or as a selection for jobs. The normal distribution of IQ scores can be represented by something called the Bell Curve, the addition of small, random variations in both genetic and environmental influences. A book by Herstein and Murray, *The Bell Curve* (1994), was controversial because the authors suggested there were racial differences in intelligence, since "it seems highly likely to us that both genes and the environment have something to do with racial differences." Less provocatively, the book points out that presumed differences in intelligence have resulted in systemic social differences, and can indicate more accurately than the socioeconomic background whether the subject will rise through the "classes". Research by Arthur Jensen (b.1923) at UC Berkeley concluded that intelligence is 40–80 per cent genetically heritable. While the research referred to above was conducted within American society, its methods can be universally applied.

Perhaps more interesting, but no less controversial, is the theory of multiple intelligences devised by Howard Gardner (b.1943), Professor of Cognition and Education at Harvard's Graduate School of Education. His theory argues that there are different kinds of intelligence. If we take intelligence to be our ability to acquire and apply knowledge and skills, Gardner proposed that both the acquisition and application can be applied to eight different forms of intelligence: linguistic, musical, logic-mathematical, spatial, bodily kinaesthetic, naturalistic, interpersonal and intrapersonal. Thus, rather than being driven by one overriding intelligence, each of us according to our personality, genetics, environment and so on will develop one of these forms of intelligence that will dominate. Clearly, also, they can impinge on each other.

Rightly directed, intelligence can be a useful marker of a person's ability. However, the debate continues as to whether intelligence can be manipulated, like genetically modified crops, to produce a regulated harvest of brilliant scientists, artists or artisans.

Why do we want things?

If we pose this question to a philosopher, a sociologist, an anthropologist and an evolutionary scientist, we will get four different answers. From them, we can extrapolate the following.

Beyond necessities, our desire for things is probably cultivated by the first presents we were given in earliest childhood. To receive a gift is pleasurable: it tells us that, for a while at least, we are the centre of someone's attention, and the more the gift is in accord with our predilections, the more pleasure it affords. From the moment we have our own money, our wanting things moves into a higher gear, and gradually we become a cog in the economic machinery. We buy "to keep up with the Joneses", to boost our self-esteem, to raise our visible standard of living above that of others. Even if we do not need many of the things we buy, these superfluous purchases especially can give us a great deal of satisfaction.

At a deeper, psychological level, why we want things is something of a mystery. As the science journalist Melinda Wenner

Moyer (b.1978) pointed out, "we may be able to predict how we will behave in particular conditions, or know that clear preferences emerge in certain situations, but we know very little about where these inclinations come from in the first place." What we call "status", taken to be our standing among our peers or in society generally, is also established by what we own – for example, the car we drive, the kind of house we live in and the clothes we wear. We want things because we derive confidence from owning them, together with a sense of security derived from knowing that what we own is within our control and management.

The whole process of wanting things can become obsessional; and when it does so, our sense of values tends to be confused. This relates to our dissatisfaction with the status quo, and not being able to settle down happily with what we have. What creates discontent and why, for other than utilitarian reasons, we want things, is still not entirely understood. Writing in the *New Scientist*, Dalton Conley (b.1969), New York University's Professor of

* * *

❝ I like to walk about among the beautiful things that adorn the world; but private wealth I should decline, or any sort of personal possessions, because they would take away my liberty. ❞

GEORGE SANTAYANA (1863–1952)

Sociology, observed: "Sociologists, evolutionary psychologists and economists all have different ideas about what drives our preferences, yet none really gets to the bottom of the issue." But the problem of our seemingly insatiable appetite for things is an old one. Erasmus (1466–1536), the Catholic priest and humanist, had this to say: "Nowadays the rage for possession has got to such a pitch that there is nothing in the realm of nature, whether sacred or profane, out of which profit cannot be squeezed."

For some, what they have accumulated becomes an embarrassment: they are possessed by their possessions – "preoccupation ... that more than anything else prevents men from living freely and nobly", as Bertrand Russell (1872–1970) put it.

Does hypermaterialism put us at risk?

The philosophical theory of materialism holds that whatever exists is either matter, or dependent on matter for its existence. Humankind's dependence on matter transfers to things and to craving for them to the point where higher or spiritual values are eroded. This has brought us to question materialism as such, and to be aware of the dangers of being materialistic. An obsession with materialism has led to a culture in which the meaning of life and its most important values rest on the assumption that nothing is valid or worthwhile beyond the range of our senses. We produce and we consume, and between these parameters we live and move and have our being.

The Swiss philosopher Henri-Frédéric Amiel (1821–1881) raged against materialism: "materialism coarsens and petrifies everything," he wrote, "making everything vulgar, and every truth false." This may be an overstatement, but it does warn against the kinds of risks to which we are exposed. The belief that ultimate value and security can be found in material things reduces and desensitizes life; it undermines other values such as philosophical curiosity, personal spirituality and qualities like beauty, peace of mind, and contentment. Satisfaction gained from materialism is short-lived, as Mark Twain (1835–1910) noted: "Any so-called material thing that you want is merely a symbol: you want it not for itself, but because it will content your spirit for the moment."

The most obvious aspect of hypermaterialism is the advanced technology characteristic of our culture, especially in the mass-market forms of computers, telecommunications, mobile phones and means of transport. There are vast benefits gained from what technology has contributed, for example, to medicine, education and all forms of research, academic and otherwise; but the question arises, are there risks involved in what technology is achieving, and do some of its applications run contrary to nature? Transhumanism is a movement that advocates the use of technology to eradicate all forms of disability, suffering, and even ageing, to the point of regarding involuntary death as no longer inevitable. To this end, research is using biotechnology and nano-technology, the latter being an emerging discpline that aims to control matter at the atomic and molecular level. Does Transhumanism, which aims at an absolute control of matter, put at risk our essential humanity? Writing in 1983, Vernor Vinge (b.1944), Emeritus Professor of Mathematics at the University of San Diego, said, "Within thirty years, we will have the techno-

" Nowadays the world is becoming increasingly materialistic, and mankind is reaching toward the very zenith of external progress, driven by an insatiable desire for power and vast possessions. "

H.H. THE DALAI LAMA (B.1935)

logical means to create superhuman intelligence. Shortly after, the human era will be ended." This technological aspect of hyper-materialism sees a human being as an artefact, and aims to assist the natural evolutionary process by redesigning it. But will this form of hypermaterialism produce a race of Dr Spocks – efficient and durable human beings that are, however, devoid of feeling and emotion?

Should we try to accept things as they are?

The search for knowledge and understanding has been a charac-teristic of humankind since the beginnings of consciousness. So intense and persistent is it, that it could be argued that the need to know is essential to our survival and that natural selection has added it to our DNA. However, this faces us with a paradox: we are constitutionally unable just to accept things as they are, but there are times when that is all we can do. The instinct not to accept is the energy behind the growth of civilization. Without the "quest" to move on from one state to another, we would still be living in caves. To that extent we're conditioned not to accept things as they are. In terms of what we learn, we would be unwise to accept something simply because it is part of a received tradition, or because we have read or have been told that something is "true", or should be understood or done in a particular way. Krishnamurti (1895–1986) warned that "any acceptance of authority is the very denial of truth."

We must, of course, include ourselves among those "things" to be accepted, and this may, for some, be difficult to do. Self-knowledge, as noted, is the key to all true understanding, but it may take the best part of a lifetime to achieve. Carl Jung (1875–1961) warns that "the most terrifying thing is to accept ourselves completely," because in the process of doing so we must face our limitations and the darker aspects of our personality. This done, we must then find, in the words of Paul Tillich (1886–1965), "the courage to be". In all things, acceptance is the first condition of change.

The need to accept touches not just ourselves and our immediate circumstances, but also what we know of the universe.

* * *

&& Our entire life consists ultimately in accepting ourselves as we are. &&

JEAN ANOUILH (1910–1987)

Science has moved us from myth and religious speculation to objective knowledge, and the process has brought about the most radical change in our personal culture, and that of our civilization. Such a change is a kind of emancipation, the mind set free to harbour whatever concepts it pleases without the risk of being ostracized, religiously, politically or socially. But as the Israelites emancipated from Egypt discovered, finding oneself free can be daunting and fearful. The acceptance of being liberated from myth, superstition and orthodoxy is proving difficult for many who have had the courage to let go of the received traditions and the theological accounts of, for example, the origin of the universe. Those faiths founded on such accounts, principally the biblical religions, have developed "schools" of thought that have tried to accommodate the information made available by evolutionary biologists and astrophysicists. For them, only the acceptance of things as they *really* are has made this liberalism possible.

Acceptance can be the way to true peace of mind. It does not imply being unrealistic, or that we are guarding a closed mind to protect a belief or a principle, or because we are afraid to face the truth. True acceptance may require stark realism which, to use the Buddhist term *tathata*, meaning the actual nature of things, invites us to see things as they really are. The Buddha taught that to accept is to transcend and to transcend is to be enlightened.

5
Spirituality

" The Soul is placed in the body like a rough diamond, and must be polished, or the lustre of it will never appear. "

DANIEL DEFOE (1660–1731)

" We are not human beings having a spiritual experience. We are spiritual beings having a human experience. "

PIERRE TEILHARD DE CHARDIN (1881–1955)

What is spirit?

The two ideas most commonly associated with "spirit" are the animating force within all living things and the notion of an incorporeal being that can manifest itself to us. The word is also used with reference to ghosts, phantoms and poltergeists, or to a power that can possess a person or a place. "Spirit" is the word used to translate the *Geist* of Hegel (1770–1831), with "mind" as an alternative. For Hegel, the spirit has "being" of itself and is therefore an "I". Interestingly, he referred to three types of spirit: subjective, objective and absolute. The subjective spirit is that aspect of a person that is independent of relationships, and concerned with ideas such as consciousness, memory, thought and will. The objective spirit is the person in relationship to others, involved with what is "right" in both legal and moral senses. The absolute spirit is occupied with art, religion, philosophy and the "infinite", which is not to be understood as boundless spirit, but one which, as Hegel poignantly put it, "returned to itself from self-estrangement". It is in this form that the three aspects of the human spirit are integrated.

Our Western culture has always made a sharp distinction between spirit and matter, thus setting up a conflict between soul and body, or spirit and flesh. Biblical religion has been so formative on our thinking that these distinctions have been heightened to the point of irreconcilable dualism. For Christianity, the body and soul are opposed entities: the body dies, the soul, given certain conditions, survives. A kind of civil war is waged in our psyche – "the spirit is willing but the flesh is weak," with the sins of the flesh endangering the life of the spirit, possibly terminally. The flesh has to be disciplined, punished, its appetites subdued, all so that the spirit might flourish and be set free.

We cannot debate here the evidence for spirits that emanate as ghosts and the like, and neither should we dwell on the Holy Spirit, the third member of the Christian trinity. Spirit as a human attribute was something originally breathed into the first man, as the Genesis myth describes: "The Lord God formed man from the dust of the earth. He blew into his nostrils the breath of life and man became a living being." The idea is similar to the Vedic *prana,* the "vital life". Animism and pantheism, the belief systems of the earliest human communities, understood that everything, both animate and inanimate, was endowed with a spirit. In this broader sense, there are many who attest to a "life force" which seems to transcend the physical forms that encapsulate it. Rumi (1207–1273) wrote: "Christian, Jew, Muslim, shaman, Zoroastrian, stone, ground, mountain, river, each has a secret way of being with the mystery."

To say of someone, "they have spirit," is to say that they have a certain strength, ebullience, courage, perseverance, even stubbornness. To describe someone as a spiritual person is to recognize that, like Hegel's "absolute self", they have come back home, having taken a journey beyond themselves. The word "spirit" may best be used as a metaphor, but it is no less full of meaning than the words "thought" or "imagination".

Can we even begin to understand what is meant by God?

The greatest obstacle to our understanding is the word "God" itself. This means so many different things to countless numbers of people, across all religious traditions and cultures, as to render the word meaningless. For the atheist, the word "God" is merely pointless, since it represents a concept for which there is no verifiable evidence. Surprisingly, the philosopher Martin Buber (1878–1965) suggested that "the atheist staring from his attic window is often nearer to God than the believer caught up in his own false image of God." In view of all the misconceptions, the doctrinal distortions, the theological gymnastics and the philosophical ravelling, using the word God to refer to something ultimately essential is almost blasphemous. In Buber's opinion "God" "is the most heavy-laden of all human words. None has been so soiled, so mutilated ... Just for this reason I may not abandon it." Buber believed that the word was so corrupted that it led to the "eclipse of God".

The philosophical theologian Paul Tillich (1886–1965) came closer than many to recovering meaning for the word "God", by suggesting that it represents "the ground of our being". At least this seeks to give back to the word something that everyone may be able to share, a common foundation, as it were, on which further constructions can be built. The problem is that all down the years there have been crusades and wars, missions and inquisitions in which people have suffered and died because of the subtle or radical qualifications applied to the God-constructions of

opposing theologies. When we consider these different perceptions of who, or what, God is, it is hard not to realize that we have
made God in our own image. Many will understand the frustration
of Rudyard Kipling (1865–1936): "The Three in One, the One in
Three? Not so! To my own Gods I go. It may be they shall give me
greater ease than your cold Christ and tangled Trinities."

It is unlikely that in a multi-religious, multi-cultural context,
the word "God" can be reclaimed in any meaningful way. That is,
we could never arrive at the kind of consensus that would give

> *" The God of theological theism is a being*
> *besides others and as such a part of the whole*
> *reality. He is certainly considered its most*
> *important part, but as a part and therefore*
> *as subjected to the structure of the whole. ...*
> *He is seen as a self which has a world, as an ego*
> *which relates to a thought, as a cause which is*
> *separated from its effect, as having a definite*
> *space and endless time. He is a being, not*
> *being-itself. "*

PAUL TILLICH (1886–1965)

confidence to the hope that we were all talking about the same thing. Probably this wouldn't matter, if certain religions set aside their mandate to evangelize, a fiat founded on the notion that everyone has to be persuaded to conform to a single, orthodox concept of God. Josephus (AD 37–c.100), although somewhat liberal for a first-century Jew, was right in insisting that "everyone ought to worship God according to his own inclinations, and not to be constrained by force." Even within the traditional forms of religion, people will follow their own inclinations, and the same would apply if we could achieve a liberal consensus on what the word "God" means. Within any theological conformity, what "God" means would remain subjective and personal.

It is often suggested that when we use the word "God", we are, in any case, really all talking about the same thing, since the huge range of meanings, even the opposed meanings, all boil down to the belief that, at the heart of everything, there is an "unmoved mover", a "first cause", a "life force", the *mysterium tremendum*, the originator and sustainer of everything.

Is there a God?

Whatever might be meant by the word "God", the previous discussion assumes that, in some way, God exists. The debate is perennial, but has been brought to the fore in recent years by Richard Dawkins' book *The God Delusion*. Those who say there is no God cite in their favour the absence of any objective evidence for a supreme being of any kind, least of all the creator God of biblical religions. In our own time, evolutionary biology and astro-

❝ I don't know if God exists, but it would be better for His reputation if He didn't. ❞

JULES RENARD (1864–1910)

physics have subsumed the concept of God by satisfactorily accounting for the initiatives once accorded to divine omnipotence. Voltaire (1694–1778) famously asserted, "If God did not exist, it would be necessary to invent him." The implication is, that if God's biography were to be written, his conception might have taken place when our early ancestors, fearful and in awe, desperate to account for the hostile environment in which they struggled to survive, and in need of help from a higher being, started to ask questions. For them, the idea of a god, or gods, manifest in the powers of nature, served as an answer.

The primitive beliefs of the earliest human beings were sincerely held, but later, more sophisticated folk have played with the possible existence of God as a way of hedging their bets. Blaise Pascal (1623–1662), the French philosopher and mathematician, is famous for his wager: he suggested that while we can never prove the existence of God through reason, we should conduct ourselves as though God does exist, because living our lives accordingly we have everything to gain and nothing to lose. Albert Camus (1913–1960) was of the same opinion: "I would rather live my life as if there is a God and die to find out there isn't, than live my life as if there isn't and die to find out there is."

However, the notion of hedging one's bets as to whether or not God exists suggests an attitude that is less than serious, and most people engaged in this debate would probably find a Providence-tempting agnosticism unsatisfactory, since agnosticism (see the question on page 167) implies an open mind.

When people say, "I believe in God," as in the Apostles' Creed, or in other affirmations, is the atheist to believe that they are all deluded? It has been said that a person with an experience is never at the mercy of a person with an argument, and that sounds like a reassuring point of view, but not if we want "proof" of the validity of that experience, so as to share it. However, it is possible that we have always been asking the wrong question, since "existence" may be entirely the wrong attribute to ascribe to the Divine. Rather than ask if God exists, perhaps we should be asking if God is nudging us, prompting us, quietly inviting our attention. Rudolph Otto (1889–1937) wrote of the "numinous", that sense of the immediacy of "the other", through which we become aware that "something" has touched us, but are not sure what it is. It may be aesthetic, or ethereal, or an awakening of part of our own selves. We may feel that we can comfortably identify this with the notion of God, even though it can only be shared with those who, themselves, recognize it as familiar. Such shared subjectivism, however well supported by scripture and creeds, does not constitute proof that there is a God. It may be that intuition provides a linking validation. As the wagering Pascal perceptively pointed out, "the heart has its reasons that reason cannot know."

Is God a who or a what?

We have some idea of how God is regarded from the modes of address used in worship and prayer: "Almighty God", "Our Father", "Lord", " Jesus Christ", and so on. When Moses asked God to identify himself, God replied, "*I am*" – in other words, He is the one that "is". St Paul used the term "Eternal God". For Jews, the actual name of God is too sacred to be spoken, and is represented in the scriptures by the Tetragrammaton, transliterated in English as YHVH, or YHWH. This is sometimes given vowels and written "Yahweh", from which the anglicized and vocalized name Jehovah is derived. Islam has "The 99 most beautiful names of God", which represent Allah's attributes. For example, *Ar-Rahman,* The Compassionate, or *Al-Muntaqim,* The Avenger. In Hinduism, *Bhagwaan* means "God", *Ishvar,* the Cosmic Controller, *Paramatma,* the Supreme Soul; and among many other names there are four that are more familiar: Brahma, Vishnu, Krishna and Rama. While Buddhists accept the existence of *devas* (beings in a higher plane than humans), Buddhism is non-theistic – that is, there is no concept of God as a prime mover – hence, the "who" or "what" doesn't apply. However, the historical Buddha had the attribute of a spiritual originator, a *Bodhisattva,* one "bound to enlightenment". He attained *nirvana* through his own efforts, and is understood to be the embodiment of the *Dharmakaya,* the unmanifested, inconceivable aspect of a Buddha, an "enlightened one". The Buddha was a "who", and a spiritual role model for his followers.

From the above it should be apparent that for some God is clearly a "who"; for others, an entity so abstract as to make attributes and qualities irrelevant. Even for the anthropomorphized forms of God there is a sense of ineffability: nouns and pronouns are employed to lasso a concept otherwise incomprehensible. The conundrum for any religion has always been how believers can hold to their faith, given the tension within a concept of God that is absolute and universal, as well as relative and personal.

Religions, with the beliefs that define them, evolve in much the same way as everything else. It is said that the genius of Judaism was to bring monotheism to the world out of cultures that were polytheistic; and that the genius of Christianity lay in the concept of incarnation, a device that made the invisible visible, the incomprehensible knowable. Incarnation is the most complete form of anthropomorphism, and one that has not only conditioned Western culture to think of God as a person, but has also made God accessible in terms of human relationships. "Our Father, who art in heaven ..." suggests a "who", even though it was a "what", a spirit, that was incarnated.

Are we "made" in the image of God?

For biblical religions, the idea that we are fashioned in the image of God has its origin in the Genesis myth of creation, but is reaffirmed by the myth of Jesus' birth, described as an incarnation. According to the first, we are told that we bore God's likeness; in the second, that God assumed human form. Genesis, however, gives a dual account of the creation of man. In chapter two (2:7) we learn that "the Lord God formed man from the dust of the earth. He blew into his nostrils the breath of life, and man became a living being." Then in chapter five (5:1) we are given man's genealogy: "This is the record of Adam's line. When God created man, He made him in the likeness of God." This account suggests that we resemble God in much the same way that a child resembles its parents.

The Genesis myth is not suggesting that our resemblance to God is physical: since Jesus tells us in John 4:24 that "God is spirit," being made in the image of God clearly carries another interpretation. Those who hold a fundamentalist view of creation will address this question positively and literally; while others

. . . .

‟ Q. 3. Wherein doth consist the image of God, which was put upon man in his first creation?

A. 1. Negatively, the image of God doth not consist in any outward visible resemblance of his body to God, as if God had any bodily shape.

2. Positively, the image of God doth consist in the inward resemblance of his soul to God, in knowledge, righteousness, and holiness. ‟

THOMAS VINCENT (1634–1678)

have taken the view that in resembling God spiritually we partake of his essential nature. Potentially, like any growing child, we are therefore able to aspire to the state of a higher spiritual being. However, we are not mere reflections or clones of the Divine: each of us is unique and, according to biblical theology, the image we each carry is a distortion of God's imprint.

Bound up with the notion of being made in God's image is a theological paradox. Traditionally, what impairs our image is the "sins of the flesh". It is the flesh that is to blame for our spiritual problems, and yet if made in the image of God, each of us is an incarnation: the spirit became flesh when the first man, Adam, was created, and again when the "second Adam", Jesus of Nazareth, was incarnated. Perhaps it is best to ignore the flesh-spirit dualism, as Gerhard von Rad (1901–1971) suggested: "one does well to separate as little as possible the bodily and spiritual; the whole man is created in the imago of God."

Eastern traditions spread the creation story and divine imprinting over a much broader canvas. For the Hindu, the creation that Brahma instigated is unfinished; and by developing spiritually, everyone participates in the ongoing creation process. The image of whatever is made is collective, a mosaic to which everyone contributes their unique tessera. Buddhists are born with the Buddha nature imprinted within them, but clouded by misconception, appetite, illusion. "Realization" and "enlighten-ment" are words that perfectly describe what happens when the individual discloses his original, pristine self.

If in some way we carry God's image as his representatives, we surely fall far short of the standard required. Whatever "image" may mean, it exists as potential. Mary Daly (1928–2010) affirms, "the creative potential itself in human beings, that is the image of God."

Is God the whole of nature?

The word "pantheism" derives from two Greek words – *pan*, "all", and *theos*, "god", meaning, "all is God." We can come at this in two ways. We can believe that there is no absolute, separate divinity, distinct from the entire universe and nature, and that everything we see, including ourselves, *is* God. Or we can believe that there is a separate God, but that he is within everything, that the whole of the physical world is an embodiment of the Divine. For this latter view the term "panentheism", or "god *in* everything", is sometimes used. As a religious belief pantheism implies a form of animism (from the Latin, *anima*, "soul", or "life"), a philosophical or religious idea that both the animate and inanimate worlds and all natural phenomena are endowed with a soul or spirit. The difference is that panentheism subscribes to the notion of one eternal, animating force, rather than many spirits. This concept of the indwelling spirit is woven into the belief-fabric of the earliest societies, and its thread can be traced throughout the history of ideas both in the West and the East. "God is the indwelling and not the transient cause of all things," wrote Baruch Spinoza (1632–1677); while the *Rig Veda* tells

● ●

❝ *I believe in God, only I spell it Nature.* ❞

FRANK LLOYD WRIGHT (1867–1959)

us that "Brahman is the unborn in whom all existing things abide. The One manifests as the many, the formless putting on forms."

The idea of the interconnectedness and interdependence of everything implies a diversity bound by an underlying harmony. Zeno (c.490–c.430 BC) offered the opinion that "God is the soul of the world, and each of us contains a part of the Divine Fire. All things are parts of one single system, which is called Nature." That God *is* the whole of nature is an attractive proposition; that God is apart, but also within nature, carries the problem of duality: God *and* something. The misconceptions caused by dualism are what most religions seek to overcome. The Indian philosopher and mystic poet Al-Kabir (1440–1518) cautioned us to "behold but One in all things; it is the second that leads you astray." Baruch Spinoza was excommunicated from the synagogue because of his panentheism. "God is all and all is God," he wrote, expressing a philosophy that was virtually a religion of nature. Taoism is probably the one "established" religious philosophy that teaches a pantheistic view of nature. It was well put by Zhuangzi, who lived around the 4th century BC: "The universe and I exist together and all things and I are one. He who regards all things as one is a companion of Nature."

The idea that God is the whole of nature, will appeal to many of us as liberating, for it sets aside institutional forms of religion, frees us from creeds and orthodoxy, and enables each of us to perceive in nature what is most meaningful to us – whether some form of transcendent spirit or a scientific or mathematical aesthetic.

Does Darwinism mean that God is dead?

❝ Where has God gone?" he cried. "I shall tell you. We have killed him – you and I. We are his murderers. ... Gods too decompose. God is dead. God remains dead. ❞

FRIEDRICH WILHELM NIETZSCHE (1844–1900)

The drama that Nietzsche recounts is part of a story that begins with a madman, somewhat desperately looking for God. "Where has God gone?" he wants to know. The parable is Nietzsche's way of telling us that God is dead in the hearts of modern people, killed by rationalism and science. The evolutionary theories of Charles Darwin (1809–1882) would have been a major theme of the "science" that Nietzsche held responsible for God's demise. *The Descent of Man* (1871) confronted the world with ideas that undermined the received traditions of the Bible, notably that God created the universe in six days, and that man, made in His image, was the climax of that initiative. Christendom was faced with the alternative idea that man was descended from chimpanzees, and God was pronounced dead, because for these and other reasons people stopped believing in Him.

If God died, so did man. Erich Fromm (1900–1980), the social psychologist and philosopher, made this point: "In the nineteenth century the problem was that God is dead; in the twentieth century the problem is that man is dead." Fromm was indicating a sea-change in our culture as rationalism and science threatened both the traditional perceptions of God, and faith, as the faculty of mind with which God is apprehended. However, what is significant is not the death of God and the demise of faith, so much as a change in our understanding of both. The death of God is the death of a misconception, and of the cultures that have generated and sustained it. Nietzsche, rationalism and science opened the door to Existentialism and secularism, and in the process what died was the cultural milieu in which the older concepts were held. For established religion the most telling evidence of this is the demythologizing of scripture, reducing the mythical element of the Bible so as to get a clearer picture of the underlying history. We started moving to what Dietrich Bonhoeffer (1906–1945) had always urged, a "religionless Christianity". It was a movement that touched virtually all religions.

The received concept of an incarnate God, with all its attendant anthropomorphisms, has given way, for many, to the notion of God as pure spirit, something that cannot be defined by theologies or contained in creeds. Such a concept is still fair game to evolutionary biologists, but it is still alive and well in the consciousness of millions. Which is just as well, since Irv Kupcinet (1912–2003) rightly asks, "What can you say about a society that says God is dead and Elvis is alive?"

Has humankind evolved spiritually as well as physically?

Ideas associated with spiritual evolution are diverse, encompassing concepts as general as a cyclic cosmology, or as specific and individual as epigenesis – the philosophical or theological suggestion that the mind houses the original creative impulse that is the source of all humankind's development.

Spiritual evolution as cyclic cosmology is based on the tradition embedded in some ancient cultures, of the Fall from a golden age carried through history by tribal memory and a mythology of an original paradise. The cycle, once completed, will return us to a "paradise regained". An example is the Hindu concept of the four Yugas or "ages" – huge periods of time calculated on astrological cycles. In evolving spiritually, humankind moves from the Kali Yuga, or the Dark Age of degeneration and distancing from God, through the other Yugas to the Satya Yuga, or Golden Age of the world, when the cycle will start to repeat. The Hindu teacher Swami Sri Yukteswar (1855–1936), venerated as a *Jnanavatar* (an incarnation of wisdom), wrote: "The dark age of Kali having long since passed, the world is reaching out for spiritual knowledge." Similar concepts of spiritual evolution on the "grand scale" are to be found, for example, in Buddhism, Mayan cosmology, and the Kabbalah of Isaac Luria (1534–1572).

According to the philosophy of epigenesis, the concept of spiritual evolution draws on the belief that humankind, both individually and collectively, participates in the ongoing process of creation: we build on what has already been created but each of us adds our own, unique contribution, the value of which is determined by the level of our spirituality. We evolve spiritually to the degree to which we are conscious of our creative intelligence, for the greater that is in focus, the more likely it is that our contribution will be original rather than imitative. Only when epigenesis is active can we evolve spiritually; when it is inactive, we degenerate. Humankind's spiritual evolution is related to its physical evolution, in the process of which our consciousness has evolved to the point of enabling our engagement with what we term "spirituality", as well as with other forms of abstraction. Writing in *Scientific American,* Michael Moyer expressed the view that, "Taken together, the evolutionary adaptations that made the garden of human society flourish, also provided fertile ground for belief in God."

When we compare primitive societies with our own, value judgments are applied to suggest that we are more advanced, more sophisticated, more humanitarian and so on. True, we have evolved spiritually from our early beginnings, and in doing so have contributed much to creation through the arts, technology and all forms of science. But our spiritual evolution has done little to rid our civilization of inhumanity; we are not less violent than our ancestors, nor are we more reverent of our environment. Put briefly, we have evolved from organically uncomplicated forms of life to become intelligent creators conscious of our spiritual potential.

Evolution is holistic. We develop not just spiritually, but on many different fronts at the same time, with complex interconnections between them. For Ken Wilber (b.1949), spiritual evolution is inextricably linked to the evolution of consciousness: "the most radical, pervasive, and earth-shaking transformation," he believed, "would occur simply if everybody truly evolved to a mature, rational, and responsible ego, capable of freely participating in the open exchange of mutual self-esteem. There is the 'edge of history.' There would be a real New Age."

Do I have a soul?

That we have a soul is, for some, our basic delusion; for others, it is the fundamental principle of life. The word "soul" is as corrupted as the word "God". As with any word capable of various meanings, we loose sight of what it actually represents. For Socrates (469–399 BC), the soul was instrumental in understanding the purpose of life: "The end of life is to be like God, and the soul following God will be like him." Socrates spoke of the need to tend, nourish and protect the soul's immortality, and Plato (c.428–c.347 BC) suggested that the philosopher was, like a doctor, responsible for the health and well-being of the soul. The Greek tradition, which had considerable influence on the developing theologies of biblical religion, conceived of the soul as our

. . . .

" You don't have a soul. You are a Soul. You have a body. "

C.S. LEWIS (1898–1963)

individual share of the divine intellect, so distinguishing us from (other) animals. This "part" of us is immortal and transcendent – something, other than and beyond mind, with which we apprehend the true nature of things. For Aristotle, the soul was the form of the body, the body was the matter, or substance, of the soul – a relationship carried through to Hebraic religion. In the Old Testament, the Hebrew *nephesh* is translated as "soul", "life", or "life breath", and the Book of Proverbs tells us, "The life breath of man is the lamp of the Lord, revealing all his inmost parts." Judaism, however, does not separate the soul from the body – its emphasis is on man as a unit of combined vital powers. The body is the soul's temple, the soul incarnate, and Christianity developed this idea, seeing the soul as that aspect of a person that survives physical death. St Matthew points to the vital importance, "What is a man profited, if he shall gain the whole world, and lose his own soul" (Matthew 16:26).

The word "soul" clearly represents an abiding, essential aspect of our makeup, something that the Buddhist *Avadanas* (tales of the saints) suggest is inborn: "Scent is the essence of flowers, oil is inherent in sesame ... and in the same way, the wise recognize that the soul is innate to man." In different ways, religions understand that the individual soul is related to, or is part of, a greater spiritual entity, such as the Platonic "World Soul", the omnipresent God, the universal mind, or Romanticism's striving of the soul to enter and unite with Nature. Rationalism, unable to accept the existence of the soul as a spiritual entity, nevertheless recognizes its attributes – namely, will, vitality, joy, mental strength and memory.

Whether it is a property of mind, the spirit, or both, we may well have a soul that survives our physical death, but on this side of the divide there is no hard proof. Even so, our consciousness of self keeps us aware of something within us that is of the essence, what Lama Anagarika Govinda (1898–1985) called "the deep and hidden well of our being", suggesting that "it's not immutability that makes our soul great, but its faculty of transformation that enables us to resound with the tunes of all the spheres of the universe."

Where does the spirit or soul go after death?

All religions teach that the "good" soul has a final destination, and some of the names for it suggest an actual place – for example, heaven, paradise, our Father's House, the Abode of God, the Kingdom of God, the City of God, Valhalla, the Elysian Fields, Avalon, and so on. Other names are more abstract – such as *nirvana*, utopia, eternal bliss or ecstasy. In contrast, the "sinful" soul may find itself in company with the Devil in the "other place", also suggestive of a specific location – the underworld, hell, Hades, the bottomless pit, Gehenna, the Abode of the Dead, Orcus, Dis, Avernus, Tartarus, Erebus, or the Scandinavian *Niflheim,* the Hindu *Naraka,* or the Buddhist *Avichi Hell.* Concepts of hell can also refer to a state of eternal torment or misery. In some traditions the soul may remain for judgment in an intermediary state, such as Zoroastrianism's Bridge of the Requiter, Catholicism's purgatory, Judaism's Sheol, the Hindu and Buddhist hierarchy of upper realms – temporary experiences where one awaits rebirth as part of a long cyclic process of birth-death-rebirth, until one gains release from the cycle.

Whatever element of our being may survive death is the element we identify as "soul", or the essential self. Assuming we do have a soul, the debate about where it goes after death rests not just on the deeper question of whether or not we might survive death, but more specifically on how such an entity might pass to whatever destination is appropriate. Any answer must consider the notion of heredity, the principle of continuity and preservation. Physically, we have no problem with this, since the genetic code accounts for the continuation of physical characteristics between both individuals and species. What is preserved is a physical or biological "memory". However, there are many who in early life recover memories of previous existences, and their experience is well attested. For example, Rabbi Yonassan Gershom, a counsellor and spiritual healer, has written of his work with people who have recalled memories of their involvement in the Holocaust, although born many years after the events. Memory, Lama Govinda (1898–

. . . .

❝ Heaven: n. A place where the wicked cease from troubling you with talk of their personal affairs, and the good listen with attention while you expound your own. ❞

AMBROSE BIERCE (1842–1913)

1985) pointed out, "is both a form-preserving as well as form-creating force." Memory, as an aspect of consciousness, the Lama argues, "seizes the still undifferentiated, pliable, and receptive germ of life as the material basis of a new individual organism." This form of continuity and preservation, known as reincarnation, is the founding principle of Tibetan Buddhism. None of the scientific sceptics who argue that God and all things spiritual are delusive have taken the reincarnation principle into account. We can, with good reason, consider the idea of reincarnation as a plausible response to our pressing uncertainties about the afterlife.

For many, the possibility that after death our soul, spirit, consciousness or memory will be reincarnated is the most satisfactory answer to the question, Are we born only to die? It is interesting to note that the concept of reincarnation lies more easily in Eastern traditions and culture than in the West. One of the reasons for this is the Buddhist teaching on karma which, simply put, is the law of cause and effect. At death, this chain of action and reaction leaves each of us with something we still have to work out, and a newly continued life provides that opportunity. This thinking contrasts sharply with the Western notion of death being a final end of the conscious life of the individual, even though that person may survive spiritually. The idea of reincarnation has been with us for a long time. "I am confident that there truly is such a thing as living again, that the living spring from the dead, and that the souls of the dead are in existence." We may be surprised to learn that the author of these words was Socrates (469–399 BC).

What is a spiritual life?

The notion of the spiritual refers to a reality beyond the physical, implying that within the sum total of the physical world there is another dimension or energy that does not conform to physical law but, nevertheless, touches us individually. The spiritual life is a personal cultivation of this energy, by which means we deepen our sense of the "other" or the absolute. Pursuing the spiritual life usually involves certain forms of practice, such as prayer, meditation and contemplation, or the more formal liturgies and prescribed prayers performed daily by Jews, Christians and Muslims. Developing a spiritual life may or may not involve religion. Our goal need not be transcendent, but may be to find a personal orientation and a sense of purpose, direction and inspiration for this one life on Earth. A spiritual life need not be theistic: it can be aesthetic, or ethical, or both. Awe and wonder may be involved, but with the result of deepening our self-perception and understanding. For many, disillusioned with the traditional creeds, theologies and practices of religion, the spiritual life is carried by the sense that, in some way, we are connected to the whole universe – an integral part of the *mysterium tremendum*, an indispensable link in the chain of cause and effect, known to Buddhists as "dependent origination".

True spirituality resides at the heart of all religions but none of them has a monopoly on it. Wearing its religious mask, spirituality is the path to salvation or enlightenment, but so hedged about is spirituality by the dogmas, creeds, theologies and rituals imposed for its development, that if a person does mature spiritually to the point of gaining salvation or enlightenment, it seems to be despite, rather than because of, the religious framework. Eastern religions offer a more fluid concept of spirituality, understood in terms of advanced forms of awareness and perception. Developing these is not dependent on the structure of a given belief system, but on the determined focus of the individual in furthering what is termed "one-pointedness", or "immediate perception". There is no invocation of the "grace of God", no mediator, no external aid, just our own will to engage in, and commit to, the process. Ram Das (b.1931) puts it this way: "the spiritual journey is individual, highly personal. It can't be organized or regulated. It isn't true that everybody should follow one path. Listen to your own truth."

It is likely that in trying to understand what a spiritual life is, and to live it, however modestly, we overcomplicate it, wrapping it up in theologies and mysticisms, enclosing ourselves in all manner of orthodoxies and authorities, confusing ourselves by making distinctions between body and spirit, the material and the spiritual, the secular and the sacred, even between good and bad. As the Nike advertisement recommends, we should "Just do it!" Kalu Rinpoche (1905–1989) tells us that "We live in illusion and the appearance of things. There is a reality. We are that reality. When you understand this, you see that you are nothing, and being nothing, you are everything. That's all."

What difference might the absence of God make?

That God is absent was first proposed by a trend, or attitude, in philosophy known as "existentialism", originating in the 19th century and stretching into the 20th. This focuses philosophical enquiry on the concept of being rather than knowledge. It places the responsibility of finding meaning and purpose in life entirely on the individual, who has only his or her experience and situation to draw on. Where previously a belief in God provided life with meaning, the secular milieu in which existentialism developed liberated our thinking so that, no longer under metaphysical control, the mind was able to cast around for other terms of meaningful reference. In this process God was seen to be absent, a notion prefigured by the famous proclamation by Nietzsche (1844–1900): "God is dead!" This does not imply the end of religion, since there have been many religious responses to the basic existentialist idea of self-responsibility, and it can be argued that Buddhism, with its emphasis on self-knowledge and the need to cut through a world that is entirely illusory, is an existentialist

❝ Now it's no longer the presence of God, but the absence of God, that reassures man. It's very strange, but true. ❞

FRITZ LANG (1890–1976)

religion. What is important is that our existence should be "authentic", that we should be true to ourselves; and in endeavouring to be so, some will hold to the presence of God while others, in considering their existence and the predicament in which it places them, will conclude that God is no longer there.

God's absence does not imply his non-existence, but his withdrawal. In the words of Martin Heidegger (1889–1976), he becomes "the God beyond God": he is absent in the sense that his existence is of an entirely different order, caught in the tension of being and non-being, yet requiring being in order to "be" God. Put more simply, God is absent because he cannot be known, since our minds are not capable of going beyond our sensible world. For this reason, the absence of God is a figure of man's solitude, his aloneness, since in the context of our individual "beingness", God is not to be found. Jean-Paul Sartre (1905–1980) wrote: "God is absence. God is the solitude of man." This was, and remains, the mantra of a secularism charged with spiritual potential. And yet for Søren Kierkegaard (1813–1855), God's absence spelt dread, or "angst", since our existence is laid open to an undetermined future that we can negotiate only through our freely chosen actions. For Kierkegaard the absent God was the secret God: "God is not like a human being: it is not important for God to have visible evidence so that he can see if his cause has been victorious or not; he sees in secret just as well."

Set free by God's absence, we have "come of age", as Dietrich Bonhoeffer (1906–1945) said we would. Not only has humankind been set free, but God also, since he is now religionless. We can examine the absence of God with a hard-won impunity, we can regard the vacated space anticipating its occupation by something fundamentally meaningful. Sartre's existentialist solitude has proved as formative as the myth of God's incarnation, of spirit made flesh. Interestingly, the mysticism of all the major religions is founded on the indispensability of solitude which, in its most profound sense, is an absence of self. With both God and self absent, they are free to return and meet each other again.

6

Religion

" Religion is the metaphysics
of the masses. *"*

ARTHUR SCHOPENHAUER (1788–1860)

" Religion is regarded by the common
people as true, by the wise as false,
and by the rulers as useful. *"*

SENECA THE YOUNGER (*c.*3 BC–AD 65)

What is a religion? .

The word has an interesting history. Its etymology is thought by some, such as Cicero (106–43 BC), to stem from *relegare*, meaning to reflect on something, to go over it in one's mind. Another root might be *religare*, "to bind fast", or "bind tight", giving the sense of obligation or a bond that holds people together. *Religio* is respect for something sacred, or reverence for the gods. An 11th-century Anglo-French word, *religiun*, meant a religious community, while in the 12th century a "religion" was a way of life bound by monastic vows, implying a belief in God as formulated by the Order's rule. A summary of these sources defines religion as a particular set of beliefs, together with the practices, rituals and devotions required by them, that have been authorized by custom or by council. We may add that the set of beliefs by which the religious community is defined, be it Christian or Buddhist, is likely to have an ethical code that will determine the behaviour and the conduct of the group.

Since the Enlightenment, the whole notion of a religion has become much broader. According to Émile Durkheim (1858–1917), a French sociologist, "a religion is a unified system of beliefs and practices relative to sacred things." There is no obligation here to a creed or authority, and what is "sacred" is left to the individual

* * *God has no religion.* *"*

MAHATMA GANDHI (1869–1948)

to decide. The philosopher and mathematician A.N. Whitehead (1861–1947) suggested that "religion is what the individual does with his own solitariness", a definition typical of the subjective "anything goes" point of view that was then emerging. The movement was away from all forms of orthodoxy toward simplicity. Surprisingly perhaps for the leader of Tibetan Buddhism, the Dalai Lama declared, "This is my simple religion. There is no need for temples; no need for complicated philosophy. Our own brain, our own heart is our temple; the philosophy is kindness." The principle of this kind of openness has had enormous appeal, liberating people to meet with the Divine in a way that is most meaningful to them. While it is by no means the whole story of his Christian beliefs, St James, in his first letter, gave a definition of "pure" religion, so unexpected in the context of a rigid theology that we might well feel he had not appreciated the implications of what he'd written: "Pure religion and undefiled before God the Father is this: To visit the fatherless and widows in their affliction, and to keep himself unspotted from the world." There is nothing specifically Christian about this, and what is said could sit comfortably within the many religions that find it helpful to think of God as "Father". The rest is social service, and being "unspotted from the world", a warning against acquisitiveness and materialism.

Religion, by any definition, has its detractors and mavericks, whether it be Karl Marx (1818–1883) deriding it as the "opium of the people", Bernard Shaw (1856–1950) with his secular mysticism, or Percy Bysshe Shelley (1792–1822) with his lyrical atheism. Ambrose Bierce (1842–1913), in *The Devil's Dictionary*, as usual has a pointed definition: "Religion, *n*. A daughter of

Hope and Fear, explaining to Ignorance the nature of the Unknowable."

Does religion satisfy a basic human need?

In his theory of religion, Steven Reiss, Professor of Psychology at Ohio State University, lists sixteen basic human needs that religion satisfies. "Religion," he writes, "is multi-faceted – it can't be reduced to just one or two desires." His theory is based on the concept of motivation – that is, the goal-orientated behaviour that defines our "needs". It is not possible here to outline all of the human needs he identifies, but a few examples will give the general idea of what Reiss has in mind: acceptance (the need for approval), curiosity (the need to learn), social contact (the need for friends), status (the need for social standing) and order (the need for organized, stable, predictable environments). Certainly, religion can fulfil these needs. However, even though Reiss asserts that each element of his theory can be scientifically tested, thus leading to a better general understanding of religion, the relational and social framework he outlines is not a satisfying account of what might be termed a religious instinct and hunger, however broadly this is cast.

William James (1842–1910), the American psychologist and philosopher, proposed that the only basis for understanding the function of religion was to examine it as experience – what he termed "religious genius". His emphasis was on personal religion, because all institutional forms of religion are derived from the experiences of individuals. Each of us has beliefs, religious or otherwise, and while some of these are beyond rational proof, they contribute to our fulfilment. James pointed to two kinds of basic need. The first is the need of the "healthy-minded person", who, instead of dwelling on the evil in the world, focuses on the good and positive. The religion that serves the needs of such a person would be open, less authoritarian, and of service to society. The second is the need of the "sick-souled person", who is driven by suffering, anxiety and the world's evil tendencies: to meet this person's needs their religion would be sin-orientated, offering the security of some form of redemptive and unifying experience. Interestingly, James gave, as an example of the former, the poet Walt Whitman (1819–1892): "Divine am I inside and out ... I make holy whatever I touch or am touch'd from." And of the latter, John Bunyan (1628–1688): "I could not rest content, until I did now come to some certain knowledge, whether I had faith or no, this always running in my mind ... but how can you tell you have faith?"

It can be said that the need for salvation, writ large in biblical religion, is both basic and urgent, since from this perspective we have only this one life in which to gain it. "Realization", or "enlightenment", the long processes by which Eastern religions enable us to disclose our "true selves", and to see "things as they really are", also constitute basic human needs. Our quest, whether by means of religion, science or philosophical rationalism, can be summed up as our need for "authenticity". We need to be able to live confidently, assured that the meaning and purpose in life we have adopted are valid. Thus, we speak of finding the one *true* God, of realizing our *true* selves, of experiencing *true* happiness, *true* love, and *genuine* fulfilment. All these amount to our need to know we are living authentically – a need that religion, in one of its many guises, may satisfy.

Can all religions be right?

There is truth in all religions, but differences in context and formulation tend to incompatibility. How sincerely a belief is held is no measure of its validity: it is possible to be sincerely wrong. For dialogue between religions to be worthwhile, the engagement must be in terms of broad views rather than specific details, and ideally concepts that are held in common. In the East there are similar beliefs within different cultural traditions. However, the beliefs of the biblical religions are defined by theologies and dogmas that make it more difficult to find common ground.

Sometimes truths blend, usually uneasily, to form a syncretism, a combination of beliefs that are not always as fulfilling as the parts that comprise it. Syncretism aims to reconcile opposed and disparate beliefs, or to combine beliefs in order to deepen the range and appeal of a religion. Early Christianity, for example, emerged from a variety of Jewish and

God made so many different kinds of people. Why would he allow only one way to serve him?

MARTIN BUBER (1878–1965)

Greek cultural and philosophical elements, while South American Catholicism has absorbed aspects of indigenous slave cultures and religious practices. Baha'u'lah (1817–1892), founder of the Baha'i faith, was thought to be the successor of Mohammed, Jesus, Moses, Buddha, Zoroaster and Abraham, and seems to combine elements of all their teachings. Sikhism, founded by the Guru Nanak (1469–1539), is an attempt to reconcile the Islam of the Mughals with Hinduism. "There is neither Hindu nor Muslim so whose path shall I follow?" Nanak asked. "God is neither Hindu nor Muslim and the path which I follow is God's." Syncretism is an ongoing process with many modern forms. Examples include Vietnam's "Cao Dai", which combines elements of Buddhism, Catholicism and Kardecism, and Nigeria's attempt to combine Christian and Islamic doctrines, unsurprisingly called "Chrislam".

Is it likely, then, that the many religions simply offer different paths to the same goal? Only in the broadest, most abstract sense can the answer be "yes". Christianity and Islam both claim to be the only religion that can lead its followers to God, and the paths they offer are therefore in conflict with all the other religions. The enigma, then, is reduced to one of the following: either all religions lead to the same goal, or only one religion is right. When dealing with truth claimed as absolute, there can only be one truth. There is, however, a way out of this impasse. Those religions that claim a monopoly of truth do so from a fundamentalist tradition within them ("fundamentalism" is a term we shall shortly discuss). All religions, even those with a dominating fundamentalism, aspire to an opposite, mystical tradition. Mysticism, which advocates direct experience of divine truth, is abstract: it does not depend on orthodoxy or doctrine, but leads the practitioner into transcendent states of mind where even if the vision given is the *form* of Jesus, of Kabbalah's *ein sof*, or of the ineffable, concept-free depth of Buddhist meditation, the truth apprehended is a truth in common. It is possible, therefore, that all religions in their mystical aspects are "right", because here they transcend their historical and doctrinal differences. Mysticism, says Elie Wiesel (b.1928), is a "way to attain knowledge. It's close to philosophy, except that in philosophy you go horizontally while in mysticism you go vertically."

Why do religions try to convert people?

For Christians, the "mandate for mission" is Jesus' instruction to his apostles to "Go forth therefore, and make all nations my disciples" (Matthew 28: 19–29). On the strength of these few words, Christianity became the "official" religion of the Roman Empire, from which base it spread across the entire world. Judaism understands that Gentiles have a full relationship with God through the covenant he made with Noah; there is, therefore, no need for them to become Jewish. Otherwise, each of the world's major religions has been active in disseminating their message as widely as possible. Islam's mission is not simply to convert people, but also to establish a world-wide Islamic state. As with Christianity, its mandate lies within its scriptures, the Qur'an, in the form of an instruction by Allah: "Say the truth from your Lord and let him who will believe and let him who will reject" (18:29). Yet history shows that conversion is not always a matter of free choice.

" An Enquiry into the Obligations of Christians to Use Means for the Conversion of the Heathens. "

WILLIAM CAREY (1761–1834)

. . . .

A "mandate to mission" is given by the originating figurehead of a religion based on the assumption that its teachings represent a monopoly of the truth. Jesus claimed that he was "the way, and the truth, and the life" (John 14:6), but his next assertion was even more exclusive: "No one comes to the Father except through me." Allah provides Islam with a similar authority, where he says, "We set down the Qur'an in Truth and in Truth has it descended" (17:105), and the Islamic way is described as "the path of manifest Truth" (27:79). Those engaging in missionary work, whether officially or as lay volunteers, must share the belief that they represent something unquestionable and unique. Given the mandate, it is difficult to resist its authority and yet remain faithful.

Put briefly then, religions set out to convert people because their adherents believe that they have a mandatory obligation to do so. From their point of view, everyone else is misguided, and since what is at stake are the eternal souls of the "heathens", setting out to convert such benighted folk to the "truth" is a service of ultimate importance, carrying eternal consequences. Two stories serve to illustrate the missionary dilemma. The first is told by

Archbishop Desmond Tutu (b.1931). When the missionaries came to Africa, "they had the Bible and we, the natives, had the land. They said 'Let us pray,' and we dutifully shut our eyes. When we opened them, why, they now had the land and we had the Bible." The second is from the Pulitzer Prize-winning author Annie Dillard (b.1945): "Eskimo: 'If I did not know about God and sin, would I go to hell?' Priest: 'No, not if you did not know.' Eskimo: 'Then why did you tell me?'"

Why do people become fundamentalists?

Fundamentalism has caused some of the world's most bitterly contested conflicts. It can be cast in both religious and political terms, but when cast in religious terms the argument almost always becomes political. All religions have a fundamentalist hard core. In the most extreme forms this rests on the belief that its scriptures – be it, for example, the Bible or the Qur'an – are sacrosanct and that interpretation must be uncompromisingly literal. Fundamentalism has developed militant evangelical initiatives in opposition to secularism and liberalism, and such are the numbers of the fundamentalist Christians in the United States that it is thought they may hold the balance of power in presidential elections. Similar movements are to be found in Islam, which has the more ambitious goal of creating a world Islamic state, governed by Shari'a law. Islamic fundamentalism is now widely identified with the political agenda of Middle East terrorism, despite the obvious fact that not all Islamic fundamentalists are terrorists.

In simple terms, fundamentalism provides people with an authoritative basis for their beliefs, behaviour and values; it offers a form of security that is beyond question or argument and provides the *raison d'être* to pursue, despite criticism and opposition, the cause it avows. In political terms this is not difficult to understand: for people passionate about their ideals, from Nazism's National Socialism to American civil rights, the motivating energy has been a clear-cut, unambiguous philosophy. In the realm of religion, people differ widely in their needs and will select their orientation accordingly. Psychologically, the security of a doctrinally authoritarian system will be attractive to those who require answers and precise directions. Religious fundamentalism provides a "safe house", in which such believers can shelter. The problems arise when they step outside intending to persuade others to adopt their beliefs, for at this point, as Sarvepalli Radhakrishnan (1888–1975) points out, "It is not God that is worshipped but the group or authority that claims to speak in His name."

The basic criticism of fundamentalists is that they appear to put their minds in their pockets for the sake of their faiths. "Fundamentalist religion is hell-bent on ruining the scientific education of countless thousands of innocent, well-meaning, eager young minds," says Richard Dawkins (b.1941). In terms of basic common sense, however, literalism poses another kind of problem, as the "happy heretic", Judith Hayes, pointed out: "The biblical account of Noah's Ark and the flood is, perhaps, the most implausible story for fundamentalists to defend. Where, for example, while loading the ark, did Noah find penguins and polar bears in Palestine?"

What is salvation?

Salvation implies that there is something we need to be saved from, and as defined by biblical religion this is sin and its consequences. Soteriology is a study of the doctrines of salvation, and across the various religions both the need for and means of deliverance, or redemption, take different forms. For Eastern religions the word "liberation" is more suitable than "salvation". For Christians salvation is the repairing of a fundamentally broken relationship with God caused by Adam's sin in the Garden of Eden. By faith anyone can be reconciled to God, since "God was in Christ reconciling the world to Himself, not counting their trespasses against them" (2 Corinthians 5:19). Judaism is more concerned with morality and the disposition to do good in this life than with the mysteries of the life beyond. However, there must be a *teshuva,* a "turning" away from unrighteousness, a repentance of the kind made on Yom Kippur, the day of atonement. It is said the Jews have been so busy trying to survive in this world that they

Three things are necessary for the salvation of man: to know what he ought to believe; to know what he ought to desire; and to know what he ought to do.

ST THOMAS AQUINAS (1225–1274)

have not had time to be concerned with the next. Perhaps this is why Moses Mendelssohn (1729–1786) recorded that "Judaism boasts of no exclusive revelation of eternal truths that are indispensable to salvation." Similarly, for Muslims, there is no theological emphasis on redemption. The purpose of life is to live in a way that pleases Allah. "To those who believe and do deeds of righteousness hath Allah promised forgiveness and a great reward" (Qur'an 5:9).

Eastern traditions have a concept not of salvation, but of liberation. For biblical religion, salvation involves judgment – that is, a person's final destination is decided on Judgment Day, when both faith and works are put in a balance that weighs the righteousness of a person's life. Judgment implies reward or punishment in the context of the mythologies of heaven or hell. The first of these is cast in the image of Eden; the latter is without a model, but believed to be the domain of Satan somewhere below the Earth, even as Heaven was located celestially. *Nirvana*, the goal of Eastern religions, is an abstract notion, a state of union with the Absolute, free from all forms of suffering. Its realization is entirely dependent on how the individual understands and works out the amoral karmic law of cause and effect.

Despite God's carefully established programme of salvation, there is a hint through all religions of the importance of self-help. The Buddha instructed: "Work out your own salvation. Do not depend on others."– a thought closely but somewhat incongruously echoed in the New Testament: "Work out your own salvation with fear and trembling" (Philippians 2:12). James Baldwin (1924–1987) should have the last word: "There is never time in the future in which we will work out our salvation. The challenge is in the moment; the time is always now."

Does evil really exist?

Western culture understands evil to be one part of an inveterate dualism that is opposed to "good". This polarity is conceived in absolute terms, and as such is represented by other, familiar antitheses: God and the Devil, saint and sinner, light and darkness, spirit and flesh. Few people today believe in the Devil, or Satan, reigning over his own domain, as an autonomous being in constant battle with God for our souls. But few can doubt that even without such personification, the malign energy we call "evil" is rife. Evil is thought of as an inclination, consciously and premeditatedly acted out, to cause misfortune, suffering and injury to others.

That there is evil is not dependent on either the existence of God or the Devil: it runs just as readily in a secularized society. Nor can evil be interpreted in absolute or universal terms, since how it is defined and how it manifests itself are relative to the morality of different periods and cultures. The burning of witches and heretics, once thought to be a necessary service to God, is today considered an evil practice; similarly with issues such as slavery, genocide or torture. Isaiah (45.7) records God claiming to be the cause of light and darkness (metaphors for good and evil), responsible for both "well being and creating calamity. I am the Lord who does all these." And this assertion has always posed a problem for philosophers, neatly summarized by Epicurus (341–270 BC): "Either God wants to abolish evil, and cannot; or he can, but does not want to. If he wants to, but cannot, he is impotent. If he can, but does not want to, he is wicked. If God can abolish evil, and God really wants to do it, why is there evil in the world?" St Augustine (AD 354–430) depicted evil as the absence of God, Carl Jung (1875–1961) as "the dark side of God", while Martin Luther (1483–1546) seemed to imply that a modicum of imperfection could act like a vaccination against the threat of a greater infection: "a little evil is a positive good ... so as not to give him [the Devil] the chance to make one scrupulous over mere nothings."

Martin Buber (1878–1965) believed that our inclination, or tendency, to do either good or evil implies that we have free will, that what we do is not caused by any outward influence but is our own conscious choice. Buber argued that "human nature, is, by virtue of man's freedom, paradoxical," and that a person "must choose and strive to become that which he truly is. He must relate himself to the world in a way that enables him to actualize his unique potential." These qualities of freedom and responsibility are highlighted by Buddhism: "By oneself, indeed, is evil done; by oneself is one defiled. By oneself is evil left undone; by oneself, indeed, is one purified. Purity and impurity depend on oneself. No one purifies another."

We can account for what are termed "natural evils" – fire, earthquake, illness, famine, plague, and so on – but why people inflict suffering on others remains an intractable mystery. Modern psychological theories suggest that cruelty is driven by the need to control and dominate, that it is built into humans as a vestigial remnant of the beliefs that led to animal and human sacrifice, and the instinct to hunt and to establish territory. Cruelty is driven by a craving for power, as Leo Tolstoy (1828–1910) suggested: "In order to get power and retain it, it is necessary to love power; but love of power is not connected to goodness but with qualities that are the opposite of goodness, such as pride, cunning and cruelty."

Why is there suffering?

Probably the best response to the question is to say that there is suffering because that's the way things are: it is built into the physical structure of all forms of life, although its mental and emotional apprehension will differ between them. That we suffer is part of the struggle to survive. For animals, lack of shelter or food, predation, and the lack of opportunity to reproduce defines their suffering. We humans, however, are alone in being able to reflect on suffering, and we suffer by anticipation. In the words of Friedrich Nietzsche (1844–1900), "to live is to suffer, to survive is to find some meaning in the suffering," and the mystery of suffering is compounded by exactly this problem of whether or not it has meaning. All suffering has a cause, not just a proximate cause, which may be illness and pain, unrequited love, frustrated ambition, economic uncertainty, fear, anxiety, and the knowledge of our own mortality, but also an ultimate cause, since suffering itself has been "caused" to exist. In Western culture, only its rich store of mythologies (for example, the Greek myth of Pandora) has attempted to explain why there is such a *thing* as suffering. The myth of Eve's disobedience in Eden provided the biblical explanation: her transgression impaired humanity's relationship with

If I had a formula for bypassing trouble,
I would not pass it around. Trouble creates a
capacity to handle it. I don't embrace trouble;
that's as bad as treating it as an enemy.
But I do say meet it as a friend, for you'll see
a lot of it and had better be on speaking
terms with it.

OLIVER WENDELL HOLMES (1841–1935)

God to the point of compromising the original, idyllic intention of creation. Suffering, as it were, was "let in". It is not to be overcome in this life, but if we can reconcile ourselves with God, its cessation is the hope of the life to come.

Buddhism has probably the most extensive response to the enigma of suffering, a response which holds the centre ground of its beliefs and practices. The "Four Noble Truths", address i) the fact of suffering, ii) the origin of suffering, iii) the elimination of suffering, and iv) the Path that leads to the elimination of suffering. This is known as the Noble Eightfold Path, and consists of right view, right intention, right speech, right action, right livelihood, right effort, right mindfulness and right concentration. The Noble Truths are penetrated by accepting that there is suffering, that it has an origin, that it can be eliminated, and by cultivating the Path.

Theologies and philosophies apart, life has to be lived, and for many it is lived in a world that has eschewed the God principle in favour of a rational humanism. In this world suffering is simply a fact of life, and the only positive response is to look it in the face and accept it. "Out of suffering have emerged the strongest souls; the most massive characters are seared with scars," wrote Kahlil Gibran (1883–1931). Acceptance is a courageous, objective and hugely healing attitude. Lesley Hazleton (b.1945), a psychologist and political journalist, wrote that "suffering, once accepted, loses its edge, for the terror of it lessens and what remains is generally far more manageable than we had imagined."

7
Belief

" *Human beings are perhaps never more frightening than when they are convinced beyond doubt that they are right.* "

LAURENS VAN DER POST (1906–1996)

" *Man is a credulous animal, and must believe something; in the absence of good grounds for belief, he will be satisfied with bad ones.* "

BERTRAND RUSSELL (1872–1970)

What is faith?

❝ Faith, n. Belief without evidence in what is told by one who speaks without knowledge, of things without parallel. ❞

AMBROSE BIERCE (1842–1914)

We may add to Bierce's definition that of St Paul: "faith gives substance to our hopes, and makes us certain of realities we do not see." But faith does not stand alone. St James tells us that it must have a practical expression in life, since "faith divorced from deeds is barren," nor is it ever far removed from doubt. William James (1842–1910) went so far as to say that "faith means belief in something concerning which doubt is theoretically possible." When Jesus assured the father of the demon-possessed boy that "Everything is possible to one who has faith," the bewildered man cried out, "I have faith ... help me where faith falls short" (Mark 9: 23–24). The German philosopher Paul Tillich (1886–1965) suggests that having doubts does not, necessarily, undermine faith, since we carry faith to our doubts: "faith embraces itself and the doubt about itself." But it is in this tension between faith and doubt that many of us live, whether the issue is faith in ourselves, in others, in the Divine or in a combination of these. Faith and doubt need each other: they cannot exist independently. Because faith is not certainty, we will, inevitably, have doubts. Doubt is simply a way of acknowledging that we don't understand everything: it is our struggle with the rational. As Mahatma Gandhi (1869–1948) asserted, "Faith must be enforced by reason. When faith becomes blind, it dies."

In Western religion, which tends towards dualism, faith is opposed by reason, whose appeal is for rational humanism rather than irrational spirituality. Despite creeds, theologies and philosophies there are no patterns, no clear maps that mark "the way" unambiguously. The poet W.H. Auden (1907–1973) suggested that "the relation of faith between subject and object is unique in every case. Hundreds may believe, but each has to believe by himself." For Buddhists, faith is one of the seven treasures (*dhanas*), a spiritual faculty and power, and one of the four "streams of merit". Faith is having confidence in the Buddha as a self-awakened teacher, and in what he taught about spiritual realization and accomplishment. But faith, of itself, is not enough, it must be rationally informed, and so the Buddha challenges his followers to go out and test if what he teaches is valid. In Buddhism there is a sense that faith is the Way, not the end; and when we follow the Way, faith is replaced by knowledge. He observed that "if one believes in the Way, such a Way of faith is the root of faith."

In summary, faith is confidence, or trust in a person or an idea. Faith in a transcendental reality of the kind defined by the world's religious philosophies is irrational, and based on assumptions that cannot be empirically proven. As St Thomas Aquinas (1225–1274) put it, "To one who has faith, no explanation is necessary. To one without faith, no explanation is possible."

Can we have faith without religion?

It is said that what a person has faith in, *is* their religion. This may be based on theism, atheism or agnosticism, and it may take the form of a theological system, a political philosophy, an aesthetic or a moral law. We exercise faith all the time, we put our trust in doctors and their prescribed medicines, in bus and train drivers, in our family and friends, also in the many services and amenities we need to use daily. Such faith is not irrational, since the trust we place draws on the experience we already have of the objects of our faith. Although we can never be sure that a doctor or bus driver won't make a mistake, or that our relationships won't founder, or that the car will start, we have discovered these dependencies to be relatively reliable, and to that extent have confidence in them. However, such faith can never be absolute.

The function of faith is traditionally defined by religion as an attitude, or disposition, that supports our belief in God, and in the ideas developed by his representatives. In a secularized society, however, it is crucial that faith is liberated from the monopoly claimed for it by religion, and from the doctrines and theologies that have always confined it. We can have faith without religion, yet we can't have spirituality without faith. John Dewey (1859–1952) made the point that "religious qualities and values if they are real at all are not bound up with any single item of intellectual assent, not even that of the existence of the God of theism." The problem has always been that in Western culture faith is conventionally applied to sacrosanct truths that define the terms and context of what is believed. Secularism has helped to blur these hard edges, and it has become possible to consider, for example, a religionless Judaism or Christianity – that is, to peel away the history, myths and accumulated theologies so as to disclose the spiritual core of the religion in question. Walter Kaufmann (1921–1980), the philosopher and poet, noted that "there are a great many religious beliefs which contain no overt reference to God, including historical affirmations, generalizations, and speculative propositions; and we may now add that there are whole religions without any god."

If we begin to wonder at this point whether a secular humanist can be spiritual, the answer is undoubtedly yes. There are trends in Naturalism, for example, that argue for this possibility – Naturalism being a philosophy that holds that all we have is nature, and that all basic truths are nature's truths. Certain responses to life that blend awe, wonder and serenity in a mixture of the emotional and the aesthetic combine to constitute a form of spirituality, through which the human spirit reaches instinctively for the transcendent. Such faith can be religionless, but this may mean having faith in a universe that is without purpose, where the physical laws accounting for existence have no other goal than to sustain it. Quite literally, the universe is a law unto itself, and exists for no reason whatsoever. If we accept this point of view, it follows that our only purpose in life is to understand this and the nature of our place within it. Such an orientation requires faith in much the same way as a religious commitment, but religionless faith implies radical open-mindedness and freedom from any established tradition. As Thich Nhat Hanh (b.1926) advised, we should not "be idolatrous or bound to any doctrine, theory, or ideology, even Buddhist ones.

Buddhist systems of thought are guiding means, they are not absolute truths."

Can we ever be sure of God's existence?

In conventional religion, belief in God's existence is a matter of faith; and in all religions faith *in* implies relationship *with*. If a person's belief in God is not based on the experience of that relationship, it is dependent on the authority of the religion itself – that is, on what is written or said. A person may believe in the tenets of a religion, but their faith will be in the authority of its tradition. However a relationship with God is conceived, certainty in God's existence will be subject to doubt. As we have seen, faith and doubt are the two faces of belief: they must exist together. Voltaire (1694–1778) understood the paradox: "Doubt is not a pleasant condition, but certainty is absurd." In any event, faith in God's existence, regardless of the depth or intensity of the religious experience, remains subjective.

Religious literature, however, contains many attempts to prove the existence of God by demonstration. Pharaoh was unable to deny the reality of the God of the Hebrew slaves when his

❝ A God who let us prove his existence would be an idol. ❞

DIETRICH BONHOEFFER (1906–1945)

existence was demonstrated in the ten "plagues" God inflicted on the Egyptians (Exodus 7:1–12) "so that Egypt will know that I am the Lord". Many were convinced of God's existence by the miracles of Jesus of Nazareth – for example, those of healing. But such demonstrative proofs seem to be confined to the periods represented in the scriptures, although some would maintain that the "age of miracles" is not dead. Damian Stayne of the Roman Catholic Cor et Lumen Christi is a contemporary healer who believes that God works healing miracles through him: "I commanded the cancers in the name of Jesus to disappear – two minutes after the prayer, there was no cancer in his mouth." Christianity has also been able to point to the occasional appearance of stigmata, the visible mimicry of the wounds inflicted on Jesus, manifested by the bleeding hands and feet of a believer. All such miracles offered as "proof" of the existence of God are interruptions if not contradictions of natural law, but this, in a sense, is a definition of miracle.

Eastern religions start from a different premise by not holding to a creator God. All forms of Hindu and Buddhist art reflect polytheism, the existence of many gods, but such representations are understood to be various aspects of the one Ultimate and wholly abstract being. Even incarnations of God or the Absolute, the fullest form of divine manifestation, are not in themselves proof.

Atheists claim to be sure that God does *not* exist, simply because there is no empirical evidence for the assertion that he does. But it can be argued that the denial of God's existence is also an act of faith. Most religious commitment is held in this tension between faith and doubt, and the Theravadan Sri Lankan monk Nyanaponika Thera (1901–1994) warned that any tendency to be sure in matters of faith "requires close scrutiny. Such scrutiny will reveal that in most cases the God-idea is only the devotee's projection of his ideal – generally a noble one – and of his fervent wish and deeply felt need to believe."

What is prayer?

Prayer, it has been said, is just the simple matter of "think and thank". But it does not always work out that way. Usually, because of its set forms, there is little thinking brought to prayer: it is offered more with the mouth than the heart and mind. But thinking, as reflection and contemplation, can be prayer in itself, a disposition of the mind toward God in the hope, at least for a passing moment, of being what Ralph Trine (1866–1958) termed "in tune with the infinite". Traditionally, two forms of prayer have dominated: praise and intercession. Praise is an expression of gratitude, wonder and worship; intercession is asking God for certain outcomes, qualified by the coda, "Your will be done." Much of intercession is a plea for support and strength, and it is said that prayer effects changes, but what may be changed most is the supplicant.

Prayer in the biblical religions is cast in the form of a mode of address – for example, in the Lord's Prayer, "Our Father, Who is in heaven ..." Whether or not that address is one-way is something of an enigma. We speak, God listens, but does he respond? Mother Teresa (1910–1997) tells us, "God speaks in the silence of the

❝ Prayer is not asking. It is a longing of the soul. It is daily admission of one's weakness. It is better in prayer to have a heart without words than words without a heart. ❞

MAHATMA GANDHI (1869–1948)

heart. Listening is the beginning of prayer." There appears to be a vast difference between congregational forms of prayer and this kind of inward personal practice, in which it might be possible to hear "the still small voice".

Answered prayer, in terms perhaps of a passed examination, business successfully transacted or an illness overcome, seems to be in the order of a miracle. God, in some way, hears the prayer, considers it, then influences events so that the prayer may be answered. Such prayer has to allow that "no" is an answer, but whatever God's response the processes involved require an adjustment of natural law. The Russian novelist Ivan Turgenev (1818–1883) made a similar point: "Whatever a man prays for, he prays for a miracle. Every prayer reduces itself to this: 'Great God, grant that twice two be not four.'" Nevertheless, the greater part of prayer is offered in the spirit of, "Ask and it shall be given." We have been "educated" to pray in terms of request, a form known as petitionary (or intercessory) prayer, and to expect practical answers in response. But prayers are not always answered directly or clearly, and that is one of the problems with intercessory prayer. One thing seems certain: whatever we ask for in prayer, we cannot just sit back and wait for something to happen, since prayer invites reciprocation. St Augustine advised: "Pray as though everything depended on God. Work as though everything depended on you."

St Francis (1181–1226) argued that "When we pray to God, we must be seeking nothing, nothing …" According to the Buddha, "the greatest prayer is patience." For Buddhists, because there is no God in the biblical sense, prayer is an opening toward truth, an unfolding of the mind. "Buddhist prayer is a form of meditation," said G.R. Lewis, a Shin Buddhist. "It is a practice of inner reconditioning … replacing the negative with the virtuous, and points us to the blessings of life."

What do mystics experience?

It is generally accepted that what all religions aspire to is realized in mystical experience. Put simply, mysticism is a conscious, yet intuitive, experience of union with the Divine, the Absolute, Nature, or whatever term is most meaningful to the person in question. Mysticism is a dynamic, an energy applied by someone who has usually withdrawn from the preoccupations of normal life, and in solitariness directs that energy toward profound contemplation, or meditation. W.B. Yeats (1865–1939) wrote that "mysticism has been in the past and probably ever will be one of the great powers of the world and it is bad scholarship to pretend the contrary." The experience of a mystic derives from a distillation of the beliefs of all religions and their doctrinal and theological formulations. It is the experience of the extracted essence of all their truths.

The common thread in mystical experience is union with the Divine. The Persian Sufi Abu Yazid (AD 804–874) described his experience as follows: "I sloughed off my self as a snake sloughs off its skin, and I looked into my essence, or self, and lo, I was He." The author of the *Bhagavad Gita* admits to the mystery of the union: "O Krishna, the stillness of divine union which you describe is beyond my comprehension." St John of the Cross (1542–1591) testifies to the fear and even agony that such union entails, for it "comes like a violent assault upon the soul to subdue it; the soul feels anguish in its weakness." The German mystic Henry Suso (1300–1366) also testifies that the mystic encounter can be challenging: "In this inconceivable mountain of the supra-divine ... where there is a precipitousness of which all pure spirits are sensible ... the soul enters a secret namelessness, a marvellous alienation ... the spirit perishes there to become all living in the wonders of the God-head."

These accounts are of an ultimate mysticism, but the experiences involved need not be quite so heightened: most of us are vouchsafed merely glimpses, often having no connection with established religions. We have already referred to the concept of "numinous", that sense of the other which may or may not be theistic. The poet William Wordsworth's experience, within which he felt "a presence that disturbs me with the joy of elevated thoughts", was a form of pantheism that has been influential in encouraging what might be termed naturalistic mysticism. Nor is mystical experience dependent on solitariness: it can be confronted anywhere, even on top of a London bus, where the writer C.S. Lewis (1898–1963) was "surprised by joy". Whether in a great place of worship or monastery, or in a cave or forest glade, or amidst the humdrum rush of everyday life, the Holocaust survivor Elie Wiesel (b.1928) tells us that mysticism "means the way to attain knowledge. It's close to philosophy, except that in philosophy you go horizontally while in mysticism you go vertically." There is something exciting about cultivating such knowledge because, as Albert Einstein (1879–1955) put it, "to know that what is impenetrable to us really exists ... this knowledge, this feeling is at the centre of true religiousness."

What is enlightenment?

Other than to describe a mental sensation of "penny-dropping", the term "enlightenment" is not used in Western religious traditions to define the ultimate spiritual experience. In our culture the Age of Enlightenment in the 17th and 18th centuries turned to reason to enquire into all forms of knowledge that had previously been the domain of metaphysics and speculative philosophy. But

❝ Knowing others is wisdom; knowing the self is enlightenment. ❞

LAO TZU (*c.*6TH CENTURY BC)

to have one's eyes opened by the force of reason, to see the truth in terms of whatever is presented to the individual, is far removed from what "enlightenment" means to Eastern religions. In the West, truth is a received tradition which, in a religious context, is disclosed by revelation. In the East, truth is something to be personally pursued, and accessed by realization. Realization happens within the mind and is validated by experience. Tenzin Gyatso, the Dalai Lama (b.1935), advises that "anything that contradicts experience and logic should be abandoned. The ultimate authority must always rest with the individual's own reason and critical analysis."

For Hindus and Buddhists, enlightenment is a refined state of personal consciousness in which it is possible to transcend desire and suffering, the obstacles to attaining *nirvana*. Such a state of mind is very subtle, to the point where Dogen Zenji (1200–1253) warns, "Do not think you will necessarily be aware of your own enlightenment." On account of reincarnation, which we will consider next, we are held in a cycle of birth-death-rebirth, and to achieve *nirvana* it is this cycle we have to break. Enlightenment is the means to achieving this. To be enlightened is to be liberated from *samsara*, the "continuous flow" of life in the mundane sense of home, possessions, family, and so on. Bodhidharma (5th–6th century) emphasizes that "as long as you're subject to birth and death, you'll never attain enlightenment."

The principal means of attaining enlightenment is meditation, a practice that comes in many forms. It can be pursued individually or in groups, it can be ritualistically formal, or entirely free of any given structure. By whatever form is followed, the practitioner will endeavour to bring the mind into a state of stillness, to arrest thought, and to eliminate conceptualization. Such practice brings about enlightenment through right thinking, which in turn enables us to pass beyond suffering and desire. It is not possible, here, to say more about the practice of meditation other than to point out that, for enlightenment, the mind is of supreme importance: it is the only tool we have with which to do the job. The Buddha could not have been clearer about this: "All that we are is the result of what we have thought. The mind is everything. What we think we become."

While the practice of meditation is basic to being liberated from *samsara,* so as to attain *nirvana,* it cannot be isolated from the life we live in the world, nor should we be over-anxious in our quest. The Dalai Lama (b.1935) advises patience: "I myself feel, and also tell other Buddhists, that the question of *nirvana* will come later. There is not much hurry. If in day-to-day life you lead a good life, honestly, with love, with compassion, with less selfishness, then automatically it will lead to *nirvana.*"

What happens when we are reincarnated?

Reincarnation is one of the most extraordinary and potentially significant religious concepts. Socrates (469–399 BC) said: "I am confident that there truly is such a thing as living again, that the living spring from the dead, and that the souls of the dead are in existence." The concept is not central to Judaism, but is found in Kabbalah mysticism as metempsychosis, or "soul cycle", and in the Hasidism of the Baal Shem Tov (1698–1760). The concept is

❝ I died a mineral and became a plant, I died a plant and rose to be animal, I died as animal and I was man. Why should I fear? When was I less by dying? ❞

RUMI (1207–1273)

rejected by Christianity in favour of resurrection, but appears in some Gnostic texts such as the *Pistis Sophia*, in which the resurrected Jesus said, "Souls are poured from one into another of different kinds of bodies of the world." The Qur'an supports the belief: "God generates beings, and sends them back over and over again, till they return to Him."

Reincarnation is most fully developed in Eastern religions and is one of their central tenets. The *Bhagavad Gita* confirms this: "as the embodied soul continuously passes in this body, from childhood to youth to old age, the soul similarly passes into another body at death. A sober person is not bewildered by such a change." Rebirth, as reincarnation is frequently termed, is widely discussed in Buddhist scriptures and usually in association with a person's karma. What we do, the way we live, will determine the "quality" or nature of our rebirth. In the *Majjhima Nikaya*, the Buddha is in conversation with Ananada, one of his disciples who has been asking questions about rebirth. To make the point about karma, the Buddha uses as illustration the extreme case of "the person who has [either] killed living beings here" or "has abstained from killing living beings here ... he will feel the result of that here and now, or in his next rebirth, or in some subsequent existence."

The principal argument for rebirth is the concept of the continuity of mind – that is, the present moment of consciousness is dependent on the previous moment of consciousness, as is the next. The Dalai Lama uses the physical world as an analogy: "all the elements in our present universe ... can be traced back to an origin, an initial point ... So mind, or consciousness, too comes into being as a result of its previous instants." Lama Govinda (1898–1985) a German monk of the Theravada tradition who became one of the West's foremost interpreters of Tibetan Buddhism, suggested that our concept of reincarnation should not be confined to a mechanistic theory of heredity, which concerns only physical characteristics, since what is "passed on" also includes a form of consciousness, talent and memory: "How otherwise could one explain that a barely four-year-old child could master spontaneously the intricacies of a complicated musical instrument like the spinet, and the even more intricate and subtle rules of musical composition, without having been taught or trained, as happened in the case of Mozart?" To this we may add the records of those who have recovered past-life memories – for example, people who have had memories of the Holocaust although born a generation later.

Reincarnation is a hypothesis whose validity we would do well to prove by our practice, by living *as though* it was true, as Nietzsche (1844–1900) suggested: "Live so that thou mayest desire to live again – that is thy duty – for in any case thou wilt live again!"

Is it self-indulgent to find spiritual fulfilment in solitude?

Finding spiritual fulfilment in solitude is probably more rare than you might expect. Even in the Eastern traditions that invest heavily in meditation, the practice is developed within the *sangha*, or community. Some individuals may withdraw for a time to follow a solitary retreat in a place that sets them apart from their society. Many seekers have sustained solitude for long periods of time, even in harsh circumstances. For example, the Tibetan Buddhist Milarepa (*c.*1052–1135) devoted himself to uninterrupted meditative practice in a Himalayan cave for nine years. In one of his poems he wrote, "Maintain the state of undistractedness and distractions will fly off. Dwell alone and you shall find a friend." Tenzin Palmo, born in London's East End in 1944 as Diane Perry, is a Buddhist nun who from 1976 spent twelve years in a remote Himalayan cave measuring ten feet by six feet, three of those years being in strict, uninterrupted meditation retreat. "The whole thing appeared very dream-like," she wrote. "It seemed almost impossible that I actually spent all that time in seclusion. It seemed more like three months. Of course, when one has been in solitude for such a long time, one's mind becomes extremely clear." In Western tradition, solitude is practised formally in the stricter monastic orders. The Carthusians, for example, are best described as a silent community of hermits, each with their own cell where they spend most of the day alone in prayer and meditation, emerging only three times a day to attend communal prayers in the chapel. Once a week they may take a country walk during which they are permitted to speak to each other.

Whether or not using solitude to develop one's spiritual life is self-indulgent depends on how it is used. Solitude implies renunciation. Enclosed and silent orders, such as the Carthusians, who renounce the world by withdrawing from it, believe that they serve by giving their lives over to prayer. The principle is true of all withdrawn monastic orders and is the usual justification given for the enclosed life – we can only assume that they believe totally in prayer's efficacy, as a tool of practical compassion. Sometimes, however, a person is "called" to solitude only so that they can be called back afterwards into the world. Tenzin Palmo admitted that she "had planned to stay in my cave, but life has a way of serving you up with what you need rather than with what you want." The Buddha, having renounced his privileged life, embarked on a solitary quest for enlightenment by becoming a hermit with rigorous asceticism. Having gained enlightenment, he re-joined society to become a teacher and the founder of Buddhism.

Most of us can only hope to have occasional periods of real solitude, and if these are inwardly renewing they are not self-indulgent. Susan L. Taylor (b.1946), the American writer and editor, said that "we need quiet time to examine our lives openly and honestly ... spending quiet time alone gives your mind an opportunity to renew itself and create order." Most people, because of the way consciousness works, feel themselves to be the centre of the world and live accordingly, assuming that their own horizons correspond with those of the world. There are few who, seeking a period of solitude and using it positively, will leave their "cave" without discovering that all their horizons have been expanded.

Is agnosticism valid?

Agnosticism, from the Greek *a-gnosis,* means "without knowledge". It is not necessarily an indication of doubt, but an acknowledgment of having less than complete knowledge. It allows a certain open-mindedness, the possibility that the agnostic may move from unsure to certain knowledge. The word was introduced by T.H. Huxley (1825–1895) in 1876, when speaking to a meeting of the Metaphysical Society – his philosophy rejected the mystical and spiritual as valid categories of knowledge and he used the term to describe his position. Agnosticism does not necessarily imply atheism, but the atheist would certainly claim to be agnostic. The term has been used by other disciplines such as psychology and philosophy to mean "not knowable" according to the present state of knowledge, a position that would change if new "evidence" or data came to light. Agnosticism can also be partial, or tentative, as for example when any assertion is preceded by, "I believe."

" *Emperor Wu of Liang asked the great master Bodhidharma, 'What is the highest meaning of the holy truths?' Bodhidharma said, 'Empty, with holiness.' The emperor said, 'Who is facing me?' Bodhidharma replied, 'I don't know.'* "

THE BLUE CLIFF RECORD (c.1300)

Agnosticism is philosophy's challenge to metaphysics and fideism, and as such has a history far older than Huxley's coining of the word. It has its origins in pre-Socratic scepticism and the philosophers of the Hellenistic Academy. How to be certain about what we know (a theme already discussed) is a major enquiry throughout the history of philosophy, examining how we acquire knowledge and the means by which we can validate it. In its broadest sense, agnosticism is not incompatible with deep religious commitment. We have seen how faith and doubt coexist, and most religious people would understand the plea of the father of the demon-possessed boy when he brought him to Jesus (Mark 9:24): "I have faith ... help me where faith falls short." Nicholas of Cusa (1401–1464), the German philosopher, even though a Cardinal and Vicar General of Rome, represented a Christian agnosticism. One of the principles of his thought was "learned ignorance", which he believed was as near as the human mind can get to knowing the truth. Agnostic Judaism is the title of a group who, although identifying themselves as Jews, do not practise Rabbinical Judaism. In propounding an agnostic Buddhism, Stephen Bachelor (b.1953) has written, "A deep agnosticism would be one founded on this kind of *unknowing*: the acknowledgement that, in terms of what life really is, I really do not know."

Agnosticism is sometimes related to what is termed "healthy scepticism", an attitude of doubt toward knowledge generally, or to a particular idea. It is a kind of suspended judgment, a "wait and see" position that sustains a "healthily" open mind until an idea or fact can be validated or disproved. Agnosticism is an exciting place to be because it suggests that the religious life, rather than being a fixed set of ideas and disciplines, is a journey of discovery. However, what we find is rarely what we think we are looking for.

Is atheism the courage not to believe?

It takes courage to be an atheist, even though it is the only rational position to adopt. Many seem to be caught in the dilemma of Voltaire (1694–1778): "To believe in God is impossible – to not believe in Him is absurd." It has been said that an atheist has as much faith as a believer. Disbelief places trust in the lack of empirical proof, belief in the incontrovertible but subjective ground of personal experience. We can understand the anonymous seeker who confessed, "I tried atheism for a while, but my faith just wasn't strong enough."

The agnostic is sometimes thought to be a fence-sitter, someone who can't make up their mind. "Don't be an agnostic – be something!" pleaded the American poet Robert Frost (1874–1963). An atheist is clearly and unambiguously "something", but more than that "something", the atheist has a message that comes with a creed and a new mission. Atheists have become courageous about spreading their Gospel, their own "good news", and in pursuit of this some of them are as evangelical as any fundamentalist Christian or Muslim. Everyone, it is implied, needs to be converted to atheism – children from primary school age through to all the State's institutions and functions. It seems that we require a baptism by total immersion in the cold, clear water of reason. And W.E. Henley (1849–1903), in his "Invictus", has already provided this "brave new world" of atheism with its anthem:

> It matters not how strait the gate,
> How charged with punishments the scroll,
> I am the master of my fate:
> I am the captain of my soul.

Such a mission, we know, certainly takes courage, and the path has been trodden before by those regimes that have tried to eliminate both religion and its adherents. Learning from history, we can anticipate what atheistic evangelism might achieve. Secular and religious views would no longer creatively co-exist, the pluralism of religious cultures would be eroded, and when it is finally proved that there is no God, and that metaphysics is merely a fanciful fairy story which can be abandoned because we have "come of age", an abiding sense of lack, together with the logic of supply and demand, would prove Voltaire right after all in saying that God, presumed to be absent or dead, will have to be invited back, or reinvented.

To be an atheist takes courage. The American political satirist, writer and TV host, Stephen Colbert (b.1964), is probably right: "Isn't an agnostic just an atheist without balls?"

Can we live by reason alone?

If it were possible to live just by reason, life would be tedious and soulless. Reason is a faculty of mind that coexists with other faculties – the emotions, imagination, intuition and the irrational, all of which combine to enable us to live in the fullest possible sense. As the critic and writer Cyril Connolly put it, "a life based on reason will always require to be balanced by an occasional bout of violent and irrational emotion, for the instinctual tribes must be satisfied." The question, however, carries the hint that not only is reason the most significant of our faculties, but that we might consider bringing reason to bear on those experiences that seem to undermine it. Reason suggests that the irrational is invalid. Martin Luther (1483–1546) believed reason to be the enemy of faith, and Benjamin Franklin (1706–1790) held that "the way to see by Faith is to shut the Eye of Reason."

This tension between reason and faith marks the kind of dualism by which Western culture is riven – "the unbridgeable gulf", as already discussed, between good and evil, spirit and flesh, and so on. The problem arises when these different modes of perception invade each other's territories. Is it reasonable to bring reason to bear on faith? Should reason encroach on the workings of our imagination; should it, for example, be the determining principle in art? It is important to distinguish between reason as the rational, empirically applied test of things, and reason as cause. If someone is, for example, a Catholic, an

. . . .

❝ The supreme function of reason is to show man that some things are beyond reason. ❞

BLAISE PASCAL (1623–1662)

Orthodox Jew or a Scientologist, that may be because of their need, psychologically, for authority and a clearly defined, answer-providing structure. That may be the reason for their specific commitment, but it is not the reason why they believe in the infallibility of the Pope, the inviolability of the Law, or in Ron Hubbard's dianetics. The reason for such beliefs is beyond reason.

Mahatma Gandhi (1869–1948), rather than seeing reason and faith in conflict, believed that reason should be brought into the service of faith: "Every formula of every religion has in this age of reason to submit to the acid test of reason and universal justice if it is to ask for universal assent." What Gandhi is suggesting is that to be seen as a valid faculty, faith, in our Postmodern world, must also be understood as a faculty of mind, as something that cannot be confined to a single defining category, such as reason, intuition and imagination, since it draws on all these. C.S. Lewis (1898–1963) wrote that "reason is the natural order of truth; but imagination is the organ of meaning." Faith is also an "organ of meaning", and, like imagination, in its fullest expression it never stands alone but always hand in hand with the truth reason has ordered.

Can intuition replace logic?

Even if it were possible, there is probably no necessity for intuition to replace logic. As with faith and reason, logic and intuition each has its special contribution to make to the apprehension of truth. Logic is a mode or system of reasoning dependent on the precise definitions of axioms. In philosophy it is the study of the structure and principles of reasoning itself, and of the soundness of argument, ensuring that every step in the progress of thought is valid. In popular use, logic is clear reasoning, the drawing of conclusions, whether in thought or debate, that are unambiguous and rational.

Carl Jung (1875–1961) described intuition as "perception via the unconscious". It is a way of arriving at the truth of something that bypasses observation, reasoned analysis or argument. However, like any other faculty, intuition needs to be informed, and both observation and reason play their part in this, as does the accumulated experience the intuitive thinker draws on unconsciously. It has been called a "sixth sense", a "gut-feeling", a "psychic radar", but it is not a pseudo-science – rather, as Immanuel Kant (1724–1804) defined it, "pure intuition is the one basic cognitive faculty, a kind of perception."

The philosopher Henri Bergson (1859–1941) said that the relative is understood by analysis, the absolute by intuition, and that for this reason intuition is the best method of understanding metaphysics. He defined it as "a simple, indivisible experience of sympathy through which one is moved into the inner being of an object to grasp what is unique and ineffable within it." As Bergson understands intuition, it runs very closely to the Zen Buddhist concept of immediate, or intuitive, perception. "Understanding," says Thich Nhat Hanh (b.1926), "is direct and immediate perception, an intuition rather than the culmination of reasoning."

For psychologists logic and intuition represent the dual brain or mind. Logic is associated with the left brain and rational thought, intuition with the right brain and emotions, feeling and the like. For most of us, the two work together to provide different possible potentials, but also, at times, one or the other side of the brain will dominate our engagement with the world. Logic, unless clumsily applied or deliberately contrived, is unlikely to lead to a false conclusion, whereas it is possible to have an intuition that may be wrong. At best, the two will work together complementing and monitoring each other, ideally in balance. Fritjof Capra (b.1939) makes this point about their complementary nature: "The fact that modern physics, the manifestation of an extreme specialisation of the rational mind, is now making contact with mysticism ... an extreme specialisation of the intuitive mind, shows very beautifully the unity and complementary nature of the rational and intuitive modes of consciousness, of the yang and the yin."

Such balance has been nicely illustrated in the naming of a mountain on Livingstone Island in the South Shetland Islands in Antarctica. Intuition Peak, it is called, in appreciation of the intuition's contribution to the development of science, and knowledge generally.

Does it really matter what we believe?

The freedom to believe pretty much what we want has spawned such an unlimited range of every kind of religious and secular system and philosophy, that there is a sense in which we are lost for choice, and thus tend to live with an "anything goes" attitude. In times past, we were told what we needed to believe, and the content of those beliefs influenced every aspect of life and culture, conditioning the way we lived, even the way we thought. What was believed was of vital importance to the individual since it determined their eternal future in either paradise or hell; and it was of equal importance to society, because the prevailing belief was a cohesive force that bound together otherwise disparate groups, providing an almost invincible authority in support of the laws and moral codes by which the populace was governed. In a sense, the clearly defined, hard-edged received tradition made life easier: people knew where they were temporally and where they were headed eternally, and for as long as they lived they had the security of an authority that claimed a monopoly on truth.

A conceptually open society is clearly an advance on the pre-Enlightenment world, but we are, undoubtedly, lost in what Martin Buber (1878–1965) called "the chaos of possibility". The emergence and spread of religious fundamentalism is a reaction to this: it is the drive to impose order on the chaos, to give some kind of clear framework where, now, none exists. The US Supreme Court judge Benjamin Cardozo (1870–1938) said: "Freedom of thought ... is the matrix, the indispensable condition, of nearly every other form of freedom." What we believe in freedom is, perhaps, more important than what we believe under

*⁣⁣ There is nothing men more readily give themselves to than pushing their own beliefs. When ordinary means fail, they add commandment, violence, fire and sword. *⁣⁣

MICHEL DE MONTAIGNE (1533–1592)

restraint, since in a democracy what determines law and morality are not the beliefs of the minority imposed on the many but the views of the individual collectively manifested.

But there is a problem with "belief" *per se,* because it can be entirely subjective, based on neither knowledge nor experience. Belief can be misguided, indeed it can be totally wrong, and it can be blindly held and perpetrated even if it has been shown to be false. "I know what I believe. I will continue to articulate what I believe, and what I believe, I believe is right," said George Bush (b.1946). Thus, the validity of belief is relative to both its content and to how and why it is shared. Niclas Berggren (b.1968), a Swedish professor of economics, has written that, "Belief drives behaviour, but often belief is not based on experience and so does not reach or reflect the intimately lived dimension of human existence." What it does do is to define identity and confer a sense of belonging. Berggren relates belief to the deeply personal compass of our lives, and sees it contributing to our sense of who we are. In so doing, he makes the important point that who we are and what we do are not entirely determined by our knowledge. Our beliefs may determine both our relationships and the way we behave. They are not necessarily final or finished: they can serve as the starting point for further inquiry, taking the form of a hypothesis, the springboard of scientific research or philosophical inquiry. The Enlightenment philosopher David Hume (1711–1776) wrote: "Belief is that act of the mind which renders realities, or what we take for such, more present to us than fictions, causes them to weigh more in the thought, and gives them a superior influence on the passions and imagination."

8

Behaviour

" *Realization of Truth is higher than all else. Higher still is truthful living.* "

GURU NANAK (1469–1539)

Do we need a moral code?

At the beginning of this section on Behaviour, it might be useful to make a distinction between morality and ethics. In common usage the words are interchangeable, but there are important distinctions. In broad terms *morality* refers to individual behaviour that may or may not conform to accepted standards; *ethics* is concerned with social behaviour, judged by the principles of an ethical system. There are forms of behaviour acceptable in private, or within a family group, that would be unacceptable in a broader context. Both words are concerned with customary behaviour, the way people do things, and both imply a standard. Morality tries to determine whether behaviour is "good" or "bad", while ethics is concerned with the study of this subject. There is a branch of ethics called "normative ethics", which sets out to determine what in a social context we should or should not do, and against this implied standard our behaviour is verified as being either "right" or "wrong". In formal terms this standard is codified as law. The question asks if we need such a code, whether constituted as criminal or common law, or enshrined in oral tradition.

We do not know when the idea of morality first developed. In the earliest human communities a sense of right and wrong would have been overlaid by necessity, and the single-minded aim to survive would have defined necessity's parameters. Anyone who behaved in such a way as to threaten an individual's survival, or that of the group, would have been seen as acting in a way that could not be tolerated, and dealt with accordingly. Eventually, patterns of behaviour were developed that were the accepted norm

– be it for a tribe or an alliance of tribes – and these patterns would have been a proto-ethic that developed as common standards for the group. From such simple beginnings the concept of "ethics" is now applied to specialist subjects, such as "medical ethics" and "business ethics". Specialist groups apart, ethics concerns all of us, as people who live among other people. In Western culture the dominant general influence is the ethical system founded on Judeo-Christian tradition, the core of which is the Ten Commandments interpreted by Jesus' Sermon on the Mount. What this represented has been absorbed by the huge and complex system of ecclesiastical, criminal and civil law that has been indispensable to the development of Western civilization.

Any society, especially one as sophisticated as ours, would fail to survive without a moral code. Without established guidelines for behaviour and the means to enforce the laws embodying them, we would be ungovernable and reduced to anarchy. As Thomas Hobbes (1588–1679) put it, our lives would be "solitary, poor, nasty, brutish, and short". To put it another way, to live without any form of moral code or ethical system would require of society the most extraordinary maturity, with everyone freely living in the best interests of everyone else. That, of course, is not possible, nor is it ever likely to be, but in a sense all ethical systems can be reduced to this principle. Put simply, an ethical system is an expression of our respect, not just for each other, but for all life. As Albert Schweitzer (1875–1965) noted, "ethics ... are nothing but reverence for life. That is what gives me the fundamental principle of morality, namely, that good consists in maintaining, promoting, and enhancing life, and that destroying, injuring and limiting life are evil."

Are there absolute moral laws?

The notion of moral absolutism presumes that there are certain actions that in any circumstances are wholly right or wholly wrong. Such laws are usually associated with rights and duties and point to a principle that must never be contravened. An absolute moral law is more likely to be found in a religious context, especially that of biblical religion, but it can also have a secular application. A law may be absolute, sometimes for centuries, but eventually cease to be so. In the Middle Ages an apostate or heretic who refused to recant would have been burned to death: the law was uncompromising. But in Western society today the law does not recognize such crimes.

The model for absolute law used to be the Ten Commandments recorded in the Old Testament (Exodus 2:17) as imperatives – for example, "Honour thy father and thy mother," "Thou shalt not commit murder," "Thou shalt not commit adultery," "Thou shalt not steal," and so on. However, each of these laws has lost the hard edge of absolutism. There is a tendency to define the absolutism of a law by the form of punishment prescribed for breaking it. In

Do not be too moral. You may cheat yourself out of much of life. Aim above morality. Be not simply good, but good for something.

HENRY DAVID THOREAU (1817–1862)

many parts of the world capital punishment remains the penalty for murder, "an eye for an eye", implying that both the law and the sanction are absolute. But the law against killing is no longer absolute, since there are different kinds of murder defined by questions of motive, provocation and premeditation. The same is true of other crimes once thought to have contravened an absolute law, such as theft or adultery.

In the West, moral absolutism is no longer defined by law but by an ideal. Somewhere within the formulations of the Ten Commandments and the endless labyrinth of law they have spawned, there is a hard moral core that cannot be whittled down. Known as the Golden Rule, it has threaded its way through our ethical systems from ancient Babylon to modern secular humanism. It is a rule of reciprocity which, posed positively, requires you to treat others as you would like to be treated yourself; and, negatively, to refrain from treating others in ways you would *not* like to be treated yourself. The Rabbi Hillel (110 BC–AD 10), when asked to sum up the Jewish law, replied: "That which is hateful to you, do not do to your fellow. That is the whole Torah; the rest is the explanation; go and learn." In Christian terms this is "Love your neighbour as yourself". In his farewell sermon, Mohammed said, "Hurt no one so that no one may hurt you." The theme is followed through in Western moral philosophy, the pivotal point of which was probably Kant's categorical imperatives. The first formulation of these is, "Act only on the maxim which you can at the same time will to become a universal law without contradiction." This is followed closely by, "Act in such a way that you treat humanity, whether in your own person or in the person of any other, always at the same time as an end and never merely as a means to an end."

The formulation of basic moral principles outlined above by Kant does not add up to an objective moral absolute, but it does represent an ideal, the lowest common denominator of civilized relationships. A moral absolute can only be held by a person who adopts it: it cannot be enforced on anyone else and remain "moral". As Pascal warned, "The world is ruled by force, not by opinion; but opinion uses force."

Should laws ever be based on religious principles?

We owe to religious principles many of the laws we obey, and while the laws have been retained, the principles are no longer held by many to be religious. That such law persists implies that its "truth" is based on values more universal than the principles of any one religion, even if those laws were originally derived from, for example, the Abrahamic faiths.

It is as if the secular society is saying, "OK, we agree that certain values are valid and indispensable and that we need them, but we don't believe in the religious sources from which they are derived." Secular humanism has dispensed with God but has retained the greater part of an ethical system based on values once believed to have been given to us by God. It shares the scepticism expressed by Blaise Pascal (1623–1662): "men never do evil so completely and cheerfully as when they do it from religious conviction." But from what conviction do they do good?

If not religion, on what might laws be based? Frédéric Bastiat (1801–1850), a French liberal theorist, warned, "When law and morality contradict each other, the citizen has the cruel alternative of either losing his moral sense or losing his respect for the law." If we dispense with religion, we have to be sure that the laws we make are morally sound, and if we cannot find an alternative to religious principles that will ensure this, these principles are better retained as the basis of law.

One such alternative is Naturalism, from which, it is argued, natural law emerges. Cicero (106–43 BC) defined natural law as "true law", which "is right reason in agreement with nature; it is of universal application, unchanging and everlasting; it summons us to duty by its commands, and averts wrongdoing by its prohibitions." By virtue of our being born human, it is suggested that nature has etched on the mind the rules of moral conduct. These include moral necessity, sympathy and basic human rights, and are implemented by conscience. Such ideas have a long pedigree starting with the Greek and Roman philosophers, but natural law doesn't necessarily set us free from religious precedent since it allows that man, "considered as a creature, must necessarily be subject to the laws of his Creator" (William Blackstone; 1723–1780). The creature, however, can only be held to have a Creator by those with religious faith, and Humanists argue, plausibly, that an inherent sense of moral law is as natural and valid as the law of gravity. Jeremy Bentham (1748–1832) a leading Utilitarian, thought that natural law was a smokescreen and that human rights were "nonsense on stilts". He claimed that "Nature has placed mankind under the governance of two sovereign masters, pain and pleasure", on which premise he advocated that whether an action was morally right or wrong should be judged according to the extent to which it minimized pain and increased pleasure. Both natural law and Utilitarianism present problems we cannot dwell on here, but as a basis for moral law they offer an alternative to religion. It is a matter of choice, but as we noted, when found to be useful, religious principles have been retained by secular lawmakers and government. Perhaps Thomas Jefferson (1743–1826) was just a touch too simplistic when, in his inaugural address as President of the US, he suggested a Golden Rule for law makers: "restrain men from injuring one another, [then] leave them otherwise free to regulate their own pursuits."

Can it sometimes be right to break the law?

The only circumstance when it may be right to break the law is when that law requires the individual or group to do something immoral and contrary to a person's conscience. Commonly quoted examples of such circumstances are the Nazi government's requirement that Jews should not be sheltered but given over to the authorities, and South Africa's law of apartheid. Although conscience is what leads someone to break these laws, such a person would inevitably be subject to whatever penalties the law demanded. "Conscientious objection" has brought people to refuse military service in the event of war, and this basis for objection has been accepted if grounded in principles of religion or freedom of thought. An objector might be assigned either a civil role (for example in agriculture) or a non-combatant role (such as stretcher-

❝ I cannot and will not recant anything, for to go against conscience is neither right nor safe. Here I stand, I can do no other, so help me God. Amen. ❞

MARTIN LUTHER (1483–1546)

• •

bearer) but would also have had the right to refuse to be involved in anything that supported the war effort.

The United Nations' Universal Declaration of Human Rights, ratified in 1948, states that, "Everyone has the right to freedom of thought, conscience and religion; this right includes freedom to change his religion or belief, and freedom, either alone or in community with others and in public or private, to manifest his religion or belief in teaching, practice, worship and observance." It can be argued that any law requiring someone to contravene these rights can be justifiably broken, and the regime enforcing such law, opposed. Conscience is a very sensitive guide. The appeal by Einstein (1879–1955), "never do anything against conscience, even if the state demands it", echoes Gandhi (1869–1948): "In matters of conscience, the law of the majority has no place."

It is possible that a law might be broken because it is found to be bad for reasons other than conscience. A law might be bad because it is unenforceable, like the law in the UK against fox hunting with hounds. To say that the law is bad is a comment on the law, not on whether fox hunting is good or bad. This law has been broken consistently, not because it is unenforceable and the police "tolerate" the hunts, but because the hunters believe that there is nothing wrong with what they are doing and that the law is an infringement of their rights and their precious freedom.

Many argue that it is a moral duty to break a law that is unjust: this is a platform for "taking the law into your own hands", always a dangerous precedent but, nevertheless, the basis of civil disobedience – itself the springboard for all civil rights movements.

In 2010, the British Deputy Prime Minister, Nick Clegg (b.1967), declared, "Today we are taking an unprecedented step. Based on the belief that it is people, not policy-makers, who know best, we are asking the people of Britain to tell us how you want to see your freedom restored." He highlighted three areas on which to focus: i) laws that have eroded civil liberties, ii) regulations that stifle the way charities and businesses work, and iii) laws that are not required and are likely to see law-abiding citizens criminalized. To what extent Mr Clegg has opened the door for law in his own country to be justifiably broken is yet to be seen.

Does karma determine our behaviour?

While karma is a term with which the Western world is familiar, it is not a concept that is well understood. It does not imply any kind of fatalism, predestination or inevitability. In Indian religions karma concerns the entire cycle of cause and effect, known as the cycle of *samsara*, manifested in human life as birth, death and rebirth. If we take the view that what we do, or what happens to us or others, originates in karma, then we are denying that we have free will and thus asserting that we have no responsibility. Karma, however, does concern cause and effect, for in an accumulative sense through numerous successive lives, what a person is today is the result of what they once were.

Karma runs at subtle levels fashioned by the concept of *samskara* (in Pali, *sankhara*), meaning "impressions", "tendencies" or "possibilities". In Buddhism these are termed "mental formational forces" or "impulses", which can be active because we initiate them, or passive because we are influenced by them. Once we are liberated from these, karma is not developed, and we enter *nirvana*. André Bareau (1921–1993), the French Buddhologist, summed up karma as a universal law in which "the deed [*karma*] produces a fruit under certain circumstances; when it is ripe then it falls on the one responsible. ... Since the time of ripening generally exceeds a lifespan, the effect of actions is necessarily one or more rebirths." Karma implies reincarnation.

How do these karmic principles touch our everyday lives? Most significantly, karma means that by the choices we make all the time, we can control the way our present life is shaped and, thus, the quality of our future life. We have no control over what we did in a past life other than to understand that what happens to us, and what we think and do, is the working out of what we once were. Our present life is, as it were, another chance to redress the negative and build on the positive aspects of our life. The Buddhist way of doing this is given, for example, in the Noble Eightfold Path: Right View, Right Intention, Right Speech and so on. The law of karma assures us that if we live our lives

❝ As the blazing fire reduces wood to ashes, similarly, the fire of Self-knowledge reduces all Karma to ashes. ❞

BHAGAVAD GITA (1ST CENTURY AD)

skilfully, according to whatever standard is meaningful to us, we will ensure a good birth in our next life. What must be understood is that we do have choices about how we live our lives, and that those choices will have a knock-on effect. Each of us is our own moral dynamic.

Two important ideas emerge. First, it is not the act or deed but the intention that determines the karmic effect of the action. If a person intends to do something good or bad, but cannot, the intention alone has consequence. Second, it needs to be repeated that karma is not a form of determinism. A person's karma will affect the nature of their rebirth but it does not affect their actions. To put this another way, karma provides a situation, it does not influence a person's freely chosen response to that situation. In using the term "situation" here I am referring to what is both general in terms of the overall context of someone's life, and particular in terms of their passage through every moment of the day. Hence the Buddhist emphasis on being mindful and on being "present" in each moment.

What are the essential values?

In moral philosophy "essential value" is usually termed "intrinsic value". Any theory of value is concerned to know what things in the world are good, desirable and important *in themselves*. Examples might include truth and justice. It's worth making the distinction with *extrinsic* value, which is something that has no value in itself but which, if applied, contributes to the value of something else. An essential value can be thought of as having an absolute standard – for example, a virtue such as goodness, or a quality such as beauty. Goodness, truth and justice all have theoretical moral value in themselves, but they also have a practical value in the form of "being good" and "telling the truth". Happiness, while it can be considered essential, is a non-moral value, but anything that advances another's happiness, such as compassion and consideration, has intrinsic value made essential by its moral content. It is easier to demonstrate that something has extrinsic value, because as a means to an end it can be measured by its efficacy – exercise, for example, has extrinsic value to the extent to which it contributes to our health. But no value can, in itself, be thought essential if the end to which it is applied is not moral in absolute terms.

Essential values are those we cannot do without. Socrates placed knowledge, especially self-knowledge, at the top of his list; while for Aristotle (384–322 BC) happiness was the greater value, since everything else, self-realization included, was a means to that end. For Plato (427–347 BC) the essential values are all bound up in the "Good Life", and there is fundamentally one, and only one, good life for people to lead. Goodness, for Plato, was an absolute, as fixed and as sure as tomorrow's sunrise. It is the ultimate governing value that is not dependent on human inclination, or on the vicissitudes of mood, expediency or desire. It is there for people to discover, but they need to be properly trained to do so. From Goodness other values arise, such as truth and justice, and it follows that "what is good" for Plato is synonymous with what is right, and that "being good", leading a good life, means living by what is right. He agreed with Socrates, that in order to discover what the good life is, people have to acquire certain kinds of knowledge. But, for Plato, the good life is not dependent on the *knowledge*, for example, of what is right, since he was also concerned to make the point that the good life can be lived out of an instinct or intuition for what is right. The problem is that while a good life is possible without that knowledge, it is insecure, haphazard, undirected. Plato's curriculum for those wanting to learn how to acquire the knowledge had two branches: i) knowledge of virtuous habits of behaviour; and ii) the development of mental power through studying mathematics and philosophy. To summarize the essence of Plato's ethical system, what is right will both determine and ensure the "business of good government", for it is with government that the responsibility of sustaining essential values rests. For Plato, the philosopher is king!

Given time, we could follow the ethical road through philosophy to see how other thinkers define the notion of essential or intrinsic value, but in a sense it all boils down to the same things: truth, justice, peace, happiness, and those conditions that ensure fundamental human rights. But note Aristotle (AD 384–322):

"We do not act rightly because we have virtue or excellence, but we rather have those because we have acted rightly."

Is there such a thing as a truly selfless act?

Altruism is an ideal, but it's difficult to determine if someone is truly altruistic, since even with the best intentions, doing something for another person can bring the benefits back to the doer. Jesus of Nazareth's self-sacrifice is frequently cited as a paradigm of a truly selfless act, yet in doing this he was fulfilling the will of God. Anyone whose life seems to be given up to serving others is likely to be doing so to fulfil something in themselves. Thus, a selfless act can never be entirely selfless. Only a few will dedicate their entire lives to serving others, but most people will offer service for some of the time, in small but significant ways. William Blake (1757–1827) put it this way: "He who would do good to another must do it in Minute Particulars: general Good is the plea of the scoundrel, hypocrite, and flatterer, for Art and Science cannot exist but in minutely organised Particulars."

In zoology, altruism is the behaviour of an animal that benefits another at its own expense. For animals, this is not a "selfless" act but something instinctual. For humans on the other hand, altruism is not entirely natural nor inherently instinctive, but an approach moved by conscience and a sense of "oughtness". Richard Dawkins (b.1941) suggested that we need to "try to teach generosity and altruism, because we are born selfish," a reference to his book, *The Selfish Gene*. Dawkins is an apostle of atheism, and the implication is that we are primarily moved to those actions that will ensure our own survival and that of the species – that whatever motive we give for what we do, we are, at base, driven by natural law.

Whether from religious or humanist principles, it is clearly beneficial to be disposed to altruism. But altruism has another dimension. If, as Dawkins suggests, it has to be taught against our inherent selfishness, we are "programmed" to be opposed to the interests of other people. What might be best for us is therefore in conflict with what might be best for others, and that being so, altruism implies that we lay aside our own interests. Perhaps only on this model can an act be truly selfless, since we must first surrender our own priorities in order for another to benefit. But the distinction is, perhaps, too precise to be made. How could Jesus have laid aside his duty to do his Father's will to the point of liberating the selflessness of his sacrifice from this secondary, ulterior motive?

The Buddhist model of altruism is the *bodhisattva*, a person who is fully enlightened but renounces complete entry into *nirvana* so

We are formed and moulded by our thoughts. Those whose minds are shaped by selfless thoughts give joy when they speak or act. Joy follows them like a shadow that never leaves them.

GAUTAMA BUDDHA (*c.*563–*c.*483 BC)

as to continue helping others to achieve enlightenment until all beings have been enlightened. And yet the Dalai Lama (b.1935) has argued, "the buddhas and *bodhisattvas* are the most selfish of all. Why? Because by cultivating altruism they achieve ultimate happiness." The point is, there is no conflict, since what moves the *bodhisattva* is compassion, and it is the cultivation of this that at the same time creates the highest degree of happiness for oneself and most benefits others. The Dalai Lama also affirmed that "Loving others does not mean that we should forget ourselves. When I say that we should be compassionate, this does not mean helping others at the expense of ourselves. Not at all."

Should we always be truthful?

Assuming that we know the truth, then theoretically we can always be truthful, and perhaps the old maxim, "Honesty is the best policy," still holds good today. The word "policy", however, draws the principle of telling the truth away from morality to expediency: it is better to tell the truth because that makes life easier and less complicated; speaking the truth, however brutal it may be, avoids the consequences of lying. The courtroom oath to tell "the truth, the whole truth and nothing but the truth" is probably a good model for justice, but outside the courtroom telling the whole truth may not be practicable, and to withhold the truth, or part of the truth, is not the same as lying. James Burgh (1714–1775), the British Whig politician, agreed: "You need not tell the whole truth, unless to those who have the right to know it all, but let all you tell be the truth."

Relationships require truthfulness, since without this quality there is no basis for trust. However, for the same reason, we may have to hold back from telling someone the whole truth: to save hurting someone's feelings, or to alleviate anxiety, we resort to the "white lie", we omit something, or misrepresent the truth so as to soften it, and this could be justifiable for someone too young to understand the truth or its implications. Such expediencies ease our way through daily life. Clearly, telling less than the truth or misrepresenting it for malicious or self-interested reasons, is ethically wrong by the standards of most societies, but usually the perpetrator will become ensnared in their own web of deceit. Lying or even compromising the truth has to be sustained, which means that lies breed lies.

While moderating the truth can be justified in personal relationships, it cannot be justified commercially. The claims of advertisements are contrived to be plausible, and even though advertising standards are quite rigorous, the "persuasion industry" by combination of image, word, sound and subliminal effects always gets across the message it wants to convey. The point is not to tell the truth, but to sell a product.

Truth is not absolute, and perhaps only physical laws such as gravity represent a truth that is unchanging – though even the law of gravity, as formulated by Isaac Newton (1643–1727), has had to be modified to accommodate new knowledge. The advocates of religion claim to be sharing the "truth" in ultimate or absolute terms, but such truths are entirely subjective and are subjectively received. All truth is flexible, relative, and subject to interpretation and modification. We deal with truths that are not clearly defined,

❝ *Scientific truth is marvellous, but moral truth is divine.* ❞

HORACE MANN (1796–1859)

and much of the time we just assume that what we hear or read is "the truth".

The extent to which we tell the whole truth, assuming that we know it, depends on the sensitivity of our conscience. Perhaps we need a marker, such as the "The Mouth of Truth", an ancient ornamental drain cover in the porch of St Maria in Cosmedin, in Rome. The monstrous face has an open mouth, and folklore has it that if you tell a lie with your fingers in the mouth, it will bite them off. Alternatively, like Pinocchio, every time someone lies we could watch their noses grow longer. Signs of our lying there may not be, but consequences there surely are.

What are our obligations to others?

Obligation often implies duty, because we have made a commitment of some kind, the terms of which make certain moral demands on us. Obligation can also imply reciprocity – for example, an act of gratitude due to someone who has done us a favour. The core obligations are self-evident: parents should care for their children, governments should rule with justice and fairness, we are all obliged to be loyal to our family and friends and to act in a way that is loyal to our principles and our faith; and, within the parameters outlined in response to the previous question, to be truthful is also a core obligation. The parable of the Good Samaritan lays on all of us the perennial obligation to respond to the sufferings of others. Simone Weil (1909–1943), the French philosopher, mystic and social activist, expressed it thus: "It is an eternal obligation toward the human being not to let him suffer from hunger when one has a chance of coming to his assistance."

Certain careers involve what might be termed "referred obligations". Those in military service are required to put their lives on the line and be loyal to Queen and country; membership to a club obliges us to honour its regulations; doctors are obliged to observe the Hippocratic Oath. All athletes taking part in an Olympic Games are required to take the Olympic Oath, and in so doing are obliged to honour it: "In the name of all the competitors I promise that we shall take part in these Olympic Games, respecting and abiding by the rules which govern them, committing ourselves to a sport without doping and without drugs... etc etc."

" Activate yourself to duty by remembering your position, who you are, and what you have obliged yourself to be. "

THOMAS À KEMPIS (c.1380–1471)

Our obligations to others are a reflection of our obligations to ourselves, and self-respect is the basis of this. The American novelist Richard Bach (b.1936) went so far as to say, "your only obligation in any lifetime is to be true to yourself." We do have responsibility, so far as it is possible, to safeguard our health, to pursue our education and careers, to work for our own happiness and fulfilment. Many fail in their obligations to themselves through the use of drugs, excessive alcohol consumption, overeating, lack of exercise, self-indulgence generally, and selfishness. In as much as we respect or neglect our obligations to ourselves, so are we sensitive to our obligations to others, and the quality or nature of a relationship can affect the claim that the obligation has on us. Failing, in respect of ourselves, may be due to our having a poor self-image. Failing in our obligations to others suggests that our relationships are impaired. When we act towards other people out of a sense of obligation, the motive seems diminished and obligation shades into duress – having to do something because it's expected of us. Such actions lack heart, even love, and can breed resentment. As Wayne Dyer (b.1940) put it, "relationships based on obligation lack dignity. If you are living out of a sense of obligation you are a slave."

Are we at fault if we can't forgive someone?

Forgiveness is written large in the biblical religions, and that emphasis has permeated our culture. What is forgiveness and how is it expressed? The Christian prays, "Forgive us our sins, for we too forgive all who have done us wrong" (Luke 11:4). Paul exhorts the

Colossians to be "forbearing with one another, and forgiving, where any of you has cause for complaint: you must forgive as the Lord forgave you" (Colossians 3:13). In his reply to Peter's question about forgiving as many as seven times someone who has wronged him, Jesus replies, "I do not say seven times; I say seventy times seven." The implications of the scriptures are that we should extend forgiveness to others because we ourselves have been forgiven, and that forgiveness is without limit or condition. For the Jew, forgiveness is one of the thirteen divine attributes, and in the *Amidah* prayer God is addressed as "the One who forgives abundantly". This is ritualized on the eve of the Day of Atonement, when it is customary for Jews to seek out those they have wronged and ask their forgiveness, but the plea is backed by an offer to make amends for the wrong done. Islam knows Allah as "The Most Forgiving", and forgiveness from him and others requires repentance. For Buddhists, forgiveness is a matter of "letting go", of not dwelling on what needs to be forgiven. "He abused me, he struck me, he overcame me, he robbed me – in those who do not harbour such thoughts hatred will cease" (*Dhammapada*).

Forgiveness is a process of healing, and failing to forgive keeps the wound festering. But to forgive, and to accept forgiveness, is not easy. To forgive is to assure someone that you no longer blame them for the issue in question, and that they can let go of their sense of guilt. If someone known to you has assaulted you, stolen from you or maliciously damaged your property, to forgive is to show them that you no longer hold this against them. But forgiveness implies relationship, it is reciprocal: it is not possible to forgive if the person injuring you is a complete stranger whom you will never see closer than across a courtroom. It is, in short, a process that ameliorates resentment and bruised emotions, and which leads to peace of mind, hopefully for both parties. Whether or not the forgiven is able to accept forgiveness and set aside the guilt may depend on the extent to which *the plea* to be forgiven is sincere. Certainly, accepting forgiveness requires us to come to terms completely with our shame.

It is possible that a person who does not forgive, who harbours resentment, will exacerbate his or her sense of injury – nothing eats away at us more than rancour and anger. However, while it may be possible to forgive, doing so can take time. In the case of family and friends, not to forgive, difficult though it may be, works against reconciliation. It is often said that we must forgive *and* forget. Sholem Asch (1880–1957), the American Jewish writer, made the point that, "not the power to remember, but its very opposite, the power to forget, is a necessary condition for our existence." Forgetting, however, may be more difficult than forgiving, and it may not be possible. Forgiveness is not conditional on forgetting: it may heal the memory, but in doing so does not erase it. That we have genuinely forgiven is measured by the extent to which the memory is no longer painful.

* *

❝ Always forgive your enemies – nothing annoys them so much. ❞

OSCAR WILDE (1854–1900)

Should we forgive ourselves?

It may be harder to forgive ourselves than others, but until we have, we may not be able to forgive at all. It is commonly held that we cannot truly love someone until we have first learned to love ourselves, but whether this is a matter of self-love or self-forgiveness, and precisely how we should achieve this state of mind, are something of a mystery. There are those who think that forgiving ourselves is part of the "new wave" self-help culture, a kind of do-it-yourself psychology that is "cool" and politically correct, and for such people it may become a means of abdicating responsibility, a way of letting themselves off the hook. It is none of these things. What is involved in forgiving ourselves draws on the most sensitive aspects of our self-knowledge, touching the strength of our compassion and the nature of our aspirations – and religion, or spirituality, may or may not be involved in this. Above all, like any form of forgiveness, it takes moral courage.

Self-forgiveness is a way of letting go of regret. How often do we find ourselves wishing we had not done or said something, or that we had decided differently about a matter of importance? Such regrets accumulate, and forgiving ourselves is the only way to dump the baggage. We need to be able to forgive ourselves, so as to move forward with our lives: not to do so anchors us in the past. As we noted previously, in order to forgive we do not have to forget. Beverly Flanigan (b.1954) puts the point well: "Forgiving what we cannot forget creates a new way to remember. We change the memory of our past into a hope for our future." As with many of life's problems, one of the keys to resolving this issue is acceptance. Whatever it is we may have done is history, it cannot be undone, and self-forgiveness begins with the courage to face up to the consequences of our words and actions. "The rule is: we cannot really forgive ourselves unless we look at the failure in our past and call it by its right name" – a comment made by Lewis B. Smedes (1921–2002). To acceptance, we have to add taking responsibility for what we have done without making excuses. And, importantly, self-forgiveness is made easier when we ask forgiveness of whomever we have wronged, and endeavour to make amends. Noel McInnis understands self-forgiveness to be central: "Since nothing can be forgiven for us that is not first forgiven by and through us, there is only one species of forgiveness: self-forgiveness."

Why is love thought to be a supreme value?

Although love has been held to be the greatest of human virtues since thoughts were first committed to writing, like "God" the word has been abused to the point of having no clear meaning. It needs to be rescued from romanticism, for while offering an image of ideal love, romance is not an energy capable of sustaining the mundane business of daily life. For many, love is almost entirely associated with sex: we "make love", we "fall in love". For others its most sublime expression is religious: "love the Lord your God with all your heart, with all your soul, with all your mind, and with all your strength." Jesus offered further guidance, "I give you a new commandment: love one another," and to Luke's account of this, John added another of Jesus' sayings: "there is no greater love than this, that a man should lay down his life for his friends" – clearly prefiguring his own death.

Love in its mystical sense is about union, as Catherine of Siena (1347–1380) understood. "Love transforms one into what one loves." Rabindranath Tagore (1861–1941) confirmed this: "Only in love are unity and duality not in conflict." Mysticism apart, our relationships with family and friends are about union and intimacy, and love is the means by which we can acquire a sense of true mutuality, of being at one with the other. It is "the condition in which the happiness of another person is essential to your own", as Robert Heinlein (1907–1988) said. Love is the means by which we satisfy an inner lack, a void, a hunger. We speak of being starved of love, of being hungry for love, as though having an inborn craving for it. This is basic, as Mother Teresa (1910–1997) noted: "The hunger for love is much more difficult to remove than hunger for bread."

The means of giving and receiving love are bound up with our emotions, and this creates a problem, since we identify love with a feeling, and if we don't feel *in* love, or feel that we are loved, we assume that love is absent. The heart and the emotions are

❝ *I have found the paradox, that if you love until it hurts, there can be no more hurt, only more love.* **❞**

MOTHER TERESA (1910–1997)

notoriously fickle and offer an unstable basis or measure of love; but to love constantly is also a matter of the will. It is, perhaps, for this reason that most forms of marriage, religious or secular, involve taking an oath and signing a contract. These are never binding in themselves, as the numbers of failed marriages indicate, but they are practical references against which an objective commitment can be made. In his paean to love, Paul wrote: "Love is patient; love is kind and envies no one. Love is never boastful, nor conceited, nor rude; never selfish, not quick to take offence. Love keeps no score of wrongs, does not gloat over other men's sins, but delights in truth" (1 Corinthians 13:4–6). For love to match any of these descriptions is primarily a matter of the mind: we *choose* to be patient, kindly, modest, considerate, forgiving and so on. We determine both *to* love someone, and *how* to love them. The supreme value of love is best expressed by a balanced combination of emotion and will, but there are no rules about how we should love, as Boethius (AD 480–524/5) said: "Who would give a law to lovers? Love is unto itself a higher law."

Further Reading

Adams, Douglas, *Life, the Universe and Everything*, Pan Books, 2003

Aristotle, *The Nicomachean Ethics*, trans. J.A.K. Thomson as *The Ethics of Aristotle*, Penguin Classics, 1956

Auden, W.H. *Selected Poems*, Faber, 1968

Augustine, Saint, *Confessions*, Penguin Classics, 1961

Batchelor, Stephen, *Buddhism Without Beliefs*, Bloomsbury, 1997

Bierce, Ambrose, *The Devil's Dictionary*, Bloomsbury, 2003

Bonhoeffer, Dietrich, *Letters and Papers from Prison*, ed. and trans. Eberhard Bethge, Touchstone, Simon & Shuster, 1997

Buber, Martin, *I and Thou*, T & T Clark, 1959

Buzzi, Giorgio, *Correspondence. Near Death Experiences*, Lancet, vol. 359, issue 9323, 15 June, 2002

Capra, Fritjof, *The Tao of Physics*, Flamingo, 1992

Cornford, F.M., *From Philosophy to Religion: A Study in the Origins of Western Speculation*, Harper Torchbooks, 1957

Dalai Lama, *Ancient Wisdom, Modern World: Ethics for the New Millennium*, Abacus Books, 2000

Dalai Lama, *The Power of Compassion*, trans. Geshe Thupten Jinpa, Thorsons, 1981

Darwin, Charles, *The Origin of Species, By Means of Natural Selection*, Wordsworth Editions, 1997

Davis, Paul, *The Mind of God*, Penguin Books, 1992

Dawkins, Richard, *The God Delusion*, Bantam Press, 2006

Descartes, René, *Philosophical Writings*, ed. and trans. Elizabeth Anscombe and Peter Geach, Nelson University Paperbacks, 1954

Eagleton, Terry, *Reason, Faith and Revolution: Reflections on the God Debate*, Yale University Press, 2009

Einstein, Albert, *Autobiographical Notes*, ed. Paul Arthur Schlipp, Open Court, 1979

Einstein, Albert, *Ideas and Opinions*, Random House, NY, 1954

Flugel, J.C., *Man, Morals and Society: A Psychoanalytical Study*, Penguin Books, 1955

Fontana, David, *Does Mind Survive Physical Death?*, Cardiff University, 2003

Fromm, Erich, *Escape from Freedom*, Rinehart & Co, 1941

Fromm, Erich, *The Art of Loving*, Harper & Row, 1956

Gandhi, Mahatma, *The Writings of Gandhi*, selected and ed., Ronald Duncan, Fontana, 1971

Gershom, Rabbi Yonassan, *Beyond the Ashes*, A.R.E. Press, 1992

Govinda, Lama Anagarika, *The Way of the White Clouds*, Overlook Press, 1996

Hawking, Stephen, *A Brief History of Time*, Guild Publishing, 1990

Heidegger, Martin, *Being and Time*, trans. John Macquarrie and Edward Robinson, Blackwell, 1993

Hobbes, Thomas, *Leviathan*, Collins/Fontana, 1974

Hoyle, Fred, *The Nature of the Universe*, Blackwell, 1950

Hume, David, *A Treatise on Human Nature*, Dover Books, 2003

James, William, *The Varieties of Religious Experience*, Signet Classics, 2003

Jeffreys, M.V.C., *Personal Values in the Modern World*, Pelican Books, 1963

Jung, C.G., *Man and his Symbols*, Picador, 1978

Jung, C.G., *Psychology and Religion: East and West*, trans. R.F.C. Hull, Routledge & Kegan Paul, 1958

Jung, C.G., *Psychology of the Unconscious*, trans. Beatrice M. Hinkle, Dover Publications, 2002

Kant, Immanuel, *Critique of Pure Reason,* J.M. Dent, 1988

Krishnamurti, Jiddu, *The Penguin Krishnamurti Reader,* ed. Mary Lutyens, Penguin Books, 1964

Lewis, Hywel D, *The Elusive Self,* MacMillan, 1982

Locke, John, *An Essay Concerning Human Understanding,* Penguin Books, 1997

Kaufmann, Walter, *Critique of Religion and Philosophy,* Princeton University Press, 1958

Maharshi, Sri Ramana *Be As You Are: The Teachings of Sri Ramana Maharshi,* ed. David Goodman, Arkana, 1985

Miner Holder, Janice, *The Handbook of Near-Death Experiences: Thirty Years of Investigation,* Praeger, 2009

Montaigne, Michel de, *The Complete Essays,* trans. M.A. Screech, Penguin Classics, 1993

Nietzsche, Friedrich, *Beyond Good and Evil,* trans. R.J. Hollingdale, Penguin Classics, 1998

Nietzsche, Friedrich, *The Will to Power,* trans. Walter Kaufmann & R J Hollingdale, Vintage Books, 1968

Nietzsche, Friedrich, *Thus Spoke Zarathustra,* trans. R. J. Hollingdale, Penguin Classics, 1961

Nowell-Smith, P.H., *Ethics,* Pelican Books, 1961

Otto, Rudolph, *The Idea of the Holy,* Pelican Books, 1959

Pascal, Blaise, *Pensées,* J.M. Dent, Everyman, 1947

Paton, H.J., *The Modern Predicament,* George, Allen & Unwin, 1958

Peake, Anthony, *Is There Life After Death?* Chartwell Books, USA/Arcturus UK, 2006

Plato, *The Republic,* trans. H.D.P. Lee, Penguin Classics, 1955

Plato, *The Symposium,* trans. Walter Hamilton, Penguin Classics, 1975

Raphael, D.D., *Moral Philosophy,* Oxford University Press, 1984

Rilke, Rainer Maria, *Selected Poems*, Penguin Books, 1964

Rogers, Carl, *The Carl Rogers Reader*, ed. Howard Kirschenbaum and Valerie Henderson, Constable, 1990

Rumi, *Selected Poems*, trans. Coleman Banks, Penguin Classics, 2004

Russell, Bertrand, *Outline of Philosophy*, George Allen & Unwin, 1979

Schweitzer, Albert, *Out of My Life and Thought*, trans. Antje Bultmann Lemke, Johns Hopkins University Press, 1998

Sumedho, Venerable Ajahn, *The Four Noble Truths*, Amaravati Publications, 1992

Tarnas, Richard, *Cosmos and Psyche*, Viking 2006

Tarnas, Richard, *The Passion of the Western Mind*, Ballantine Books, 1991

Teilhard de Chardin, Pierre, *The Phenomenon of Man*, Collins Fount Paperback, 1959

Thoreau, Henry David, *Walden*, Everyman, 1955

Tillich, Paul, *The Courage to Be*, Collins Fontana, 1965

Trungpa, Rinpoche Chogyam, *Cutting through Spiritual Materialism*, Shambhala Classics, 2002

Trungpa, Rinpoche Chogyam, *The Heart of the Buddha*, Shambhala, 1991

Tucker, Dr Jim B., *Life Before Life*, Piatkus, 2005

Voltaire, *Treatise on Tolerance and Other Writings*, trans. and ed. Simon Harvey, Cambridge University Press, 2000

Whitehead, Alfred North, *Adventures of Ideas*, Pelican, 1948

Wiesel, Eli, *Night*, Hill and Wang, 1958

Zukav, Gary, *The Dancing WuLi Masters: An Overview of the New Physics*, Bantam Books, 1980

Index

References to quotations are in *italics*

Acknowledgments

Many thanks to Michael Mann, my commissioning editor, for steering this project to contract, and to him and Penny Stopa for leading me through the several revisions of the book's structure to this stronger form.

I am particularly grateful to Bob Saxton for his rigorous scrutiny of the text and for an editing process through which I've learned new things about both the subject matter and the craft of writing.

Melinda Wenner Moyer generously allowed me to use material for "Why do we want things?" from the "Live Science" website (www.livescience.com) and from her related article in *Scientific American*. Anne Rice kindly agreed to let me quote material from her book *Vampire Diaries*, for use in responding to the question "What do we need to know?"

Every effort has been made to secure permission to reproduce material protected by copyright, and in future printings of this book I will be pleased to make good any omissions brought to my attention.

GERALD BENEDICT, PAYRIGNAC, FRANCE, JANUARY 2011